Mindblindness

$\underset{\mathscr{E}CC}{LD}$ Learning, Development, and Conceptual Change

Lila Gleitman, Susan Carey, Elissa Newport, and Elizabeth Spelke, editors

John Macnamara, *Names for Things: A Study in Human Learning* (1982)

Susan Carey, *Conceptual Change in Childhood* (1985)

David Premack, *"Gavagai!" or the Future History of the Animal Language Controversy* (1986)

Daniel N. Osherson, *Systems That Learn: An Introduction to Learning Theory for Cognitive and Computer Scientists* (1986)

James L. Morgan, *From Simple Input to Complex Grammar* (1986)

Frank C. Keil, *Concepts, Kinds, and Cognitive Development* (1989)

Steven Pinker, *Learnability and Cognition: The Acquisition of Argument Structure* (1989)

Kurt VanLehn, *Mind Bugs: The Origins of Procedural Misconception* (1990)

Ellen M. Markman, *Categorization and Naming in Children: Problems of Induction* (1990)

Henry M. Wellman, *The Child's Theory of Mind* (1990)

Charles R. Gallistel, *The Organization of Learning* (1990)

Josef Perner, *Understanding the Representational Mind* (1991)

Eleanor J. Gibson, *An Odyssey in Learning and Perception* (1991)

Annette Karmiloff-Smith, *Beyond Modularity: A Developmental Perspective on Cognitive Science* (1992)

Simon Baron-Cohen, *Mindblindness: An Essay on Autism and Theory of Mind* (1995)

Mindblindness

An Essay on Autism and Theory of Mind

Simon Baron-Cohen

A Bradford Book
The MIT Press
Cambridge, Massachusetts
London, England

Sixth printing, 1999

First MIT Press paperback edition, 1997

© 1995 Massachusetts Institute of Technology

Set in Palatino by The MIT Press.

Printed and bound in the United States of America.

Library of Congress Cataloging-in-Publication Data

Baron-Cohen, Simon
  Mindblindness: an essay on autism and theory of mind / Simon
  Baron-Cohen
    p.   cm.—(Learning, development, and conceptual change)
  "A Bradford book."
  Includes bibliographical references and index.
  ISBN 0-262-02384-9 (hb); 0-262-52225-X
    1. Human information processing. 2. Philosophy of mind. 3. Genetic
  psychology. 4. Autism. I. Title. II. Series.
  BF444.B37   1995
  616.89'82—dc20   94-36470
                                                                         CIP

I have no serious doubt that this theory (what I call "common-sense belief/desire psychology") is pretty close to being true. My reason for believing this . . . is that commonsense belief/desire psychology explains vastly more of the facts about behaviour than any of the alternative theories available. It could hardly fail to do so: there are no alternative theories available. (Fodor 1983, p. x)

Contents

Series Foreword

This series will include state-of-the-art reference works, seminal monographs, and texts on the development of concepts and mental structures. It will span domains of knowledge from syntax to geometry to the social world, and it will be concerned with all phases of development, from infancy through adulthood.

The series intends to engage these fundamental questions:

> • the nature and limits of learning and maturation: the influence of the environment, of initial structures, and of maturational changes in the nervous system on human development; learnability theory; the problem of induction; domain-specific constraints on development
> • the nature of conceptual change: conceptual organization and conceptual change in child development, in the acquisition of expertise, and in the history of science.

Lila Gleitman
Susan Carey
Elissa Newport
Elizabeth Spelke

Foreword

Just as common sense is the faculty that tells us that the world is flat, so too it tells us many other things that are equally unreliable. It tells us, for example, that color is out there in the world, an independent property of the objects we live among. But scientific investigations have led us, logical step by logical step, to escape our fanatically insistent, inelastic intuitions. As a result, we know now that color is not already out there, an inherent attribute of objects. We know this because we sometimes see physically identical objects or spectral arrays as having different colors—depending on background, circumstance, and context— and we routinely see physically different spectral arrays as having the same color. The machinery that causes these experiences allows us to identify something as the same object across situations despite the different wavelength composites that it reflects from circumstance to circumstance. Far from being a physical property of objects, color is a mental property—a useful invention that specialized circuitry computes in our minds and then "projects onto" our percepts of physically colorless objects. This invention allows us to identify and interact with objects and the world far more richly that we otherwise could. That objects seem to be colored is an invention of natural selection, which built into some species, including our own, the specialized neural circuitry responsible.

What is true for color is true for everything in our experienced worlds: the warmth of a smile, the meaning of a glance, the heft of a book, the force of a glare. Although it is a modern truism to say that we live in culturally constructed worlds, the thin surface of cultural construction is dwarfed by (and made possible by) the deep underlying strata of evolved species-typical cognitive construction. We inhabit mental worlds populated by the computational outputs of battalions of evolved, specialized neural automata. They segment words out of a continual auditory flow, they construct a world of local objects from edges and gradients in our two-dimensional retinal arrays, they infer the purpose of a hook from its shape, they recognize and make us feel the negative response of a conversational partner from the roll of her eyes, they identify cooperative intentions among individuals from their joint attention and common emotional responses, and so on.

Each of the neural automata responsible for these constructions is the carefully crafted product of thousands or millions of generations of natural selection, and each makes its own distinctive contribution to the cognitive model of the world that we individually experience as reality. Because these devices are present in all human minds, much of what they construct is the same for all people, from whatever culture; the representations produced by these universal mechanisms thereby constitute the foundation of our shared reality and our ability to communicate. Yet, because these evolved inference engines operate so automatically, we remain unaware of them and their ceaseless, silent, invisible operations. Oblivious to their existence, we mistake the representations they construct (the color of a leaf, the irony in a tone of voice, the approval of our friends, and so on) for the world itself—a world that reveals itself, unproblematically, through our senses.

Indeed, it is exactly because of their universal and automatic character that we have been blind to the existence of the machinery that constitutes most of the evolved architecture of the human mind—what might reasonably be called our cognitive instincts. Instinct blindness is sanity for the individual, but it has been crippling for scientific psychology. Scientists do not conduct research to find things whose existence they don't suspect. These mechanisms solve the many computational problems involved in constructing the world we deal with so automatically that the scientific community remained unaware for decades that these computational problems existed and were being solved as part of the ordinary functioning of the mind of every normal human being. As a consequence, most of psychology retained its empiricist orientation throughout the 20th century, resting on the assumption that a pre-packaged "world" acted though the senses and through general-purpose learning mechanisms to build our concepts, interpretative frameworks, and mental organization.

In the last two decades, though, scientific psychology has finally begun to slip the bonds imposed by this seductive but misdirecting folk psychology. Cognitive scientists were awakened by a series of encounters with alien minds, whose starkly contrasting designs and surprising incapacities drew attention to previously overlooked natural human competences and to the computational problems they routinely solve. They encountered artificial mentalities in the computer lab that had obstinate difficulties in seeing, speaking, handling objects, understanding, or doing almost anything that humans do effortlessly. They encountered thousands of animal species each of which could solve a striking diversity of natural information-processing problems that other species could not. They encountered the developing minds of infants and children, which forced them to confront the intractable computational and philosophical problems that plague empiricist models of how children acquire knowledge. And they encountered neurologically impaired individuals who displayed unanticipated dissociations of cognitive deficits and abilities. These and a host of other factors alerted psychologists to the necessity for—and to the actuality of—a vast nonconscious realm of evolved, specialized, computational problem solvers that construct and interpret the world.

Instead of viewing the world as the force that organizes the mind, researchers now view the mind as imposing (on an infinitely rich and extensive world) its own pre-existing kinds of organization—kinds invented by natural selection during the species' evolutionary history to produce adaptive ends in the species' natural environment. On this view, our cognitive architecture resembles a confederation of hundreds or thousands of functionally dedicated computers (often called modules) designed to solve adaptive problems endemic to our hunter-gatherer ancestors. Each of these devices has its own agenda and imposes its own exotic organization on different fragments of the world. There are specialized systems for grammar induction, for face recognition, for dead reckoning, for construing objects, and for recognizing emotions from the face. There are mechanisms to detect animacy, eye direction, and cheating. There is a "theory of mind" module, and a multitude of other elegant machines.

These modules appear to be structured very differently from the general-purpose cognitive machinery—"attention," "short-term memory," "category induction," and so on—proposed in the previous generation of models of the mind. In order to solve its characteristic domain of problems, a module is designed to interpret the world in its own pre-existing terms and framework, operating primarily or solely with its own specialized "lexicon"—a set of procedures, formats, and representational primitives closely tailored to the demands of its targeted family of problem. These are the languages of the human mind: diagnostic facial-muscle configurations defined by an emotion-recognition system that maps the facial expressions of others onto models of their internal states; a language-acquisition device whose conceptual primitives include elements such as "noun phrase" and "verb phrase"; a rigid object mechanics that construes the world in terms of "solid objects," relative location, and mutual exclusivity within volume boundaries; social-exchange algorithms that define a social world of agents, benefits, requirements, contingency, and cheating; and—the focus of this book—a "theory of mind" module that speaks of agents, beliefs, and desires and links them to a language of the eyes. This language is generated by still other mechanisms that detect eye direction and feed the data into a variety of social inference modules.

The realization that the human mind is densely multimodular has propelled modern psychology into a new theoretical landscape that is strikingly different from the standard empiricist approaches of the past. In consequence, the outlines of the psychological science of the coming century are getting clearer.

In this new phase of the cognitive revolution, discovering and mapping the various functionally specialized modules of the human brain will be primary activities. Even more fundamentally, psychologists are starting to put considerable effort into making their theories and findings consistent with the rest of the natural sciences, including developmental biology, biochemistry, physics, genetics, ecology, and evolutionary biology: Psychology is finally becoming a genuine natural science.

The cognitive revolution solved many of the ontological problems that had prevented psychological concepts from being located with respect to the other sciences. (What manner of thing, after all, was a mental image or an inference or a goal, next to oxidation or mass or receptor sites?) As a result, the psychological architecture can now be mapped—simultaneously and complementarily—as a system of computational relationships and as a physical system that implements these relationships. As the operation of the genetic code is tracked through molecular biology and cell biology to developmental neurobiology, the processes that organize the developing nervous system are becoming increasingly intelligible. These developmental programs were "designed" by selection to build a physical structure that realizes certain functional informational relationships. Discovering what these relationships are is the province of still other fields, such as evolutionary biology and cognitive psychology.

One of the most significant trends in the naturalization of the psychological sciences is the application of data and conceptual tools forged in evolutionary biology, behavioral ecology, primatology, and human paleoanthropology. These fields have begun to contribute an increasingly detailed list of the native information-processing functions that the human brain was built to execute. Detailed theories of adaptive function can tell cognitive scientists what modules are likely to exist, what adaptive information-processing problems they must be capable of solving, and—since form follows function—what kind of design features they can therefore be expected to have. Evolutionary biology and related fields can supply this wealth of guidance because natural selection is the only known natural process that builds functional organization into the species-typical designs of organisms. Consequently, all reliably developing functional mechanisms in a species' psychological architecture must (1) be ascribed to the operation of natural selection, (2) be consistent with its principles, and indeed (3) be organized and specifically designed to solve the narrowly identifiable sets of biological information-processing problems defined by selection operating within the context of a species' ancestral mode of life. For humans, of course, this means the world of ancestral hunter-gatherers, foraging hominids, and even pre-hominid primates.

Simon Baron-Cohen's trailblazing research gives us a preview of what psychological science will look like in the new century. In this conversational, understated volume, he attacks some of the most fundamental questions about how human beings mentally construct their commonly inhabited social world. He explores how a universal, evolved language of the eyes, which is mutually intelligible to all members of our species, can bring two separate minds into an aligned interpretation of their interaction. What we take for granted—the achievement of coordinated models of our mutual social interactions—he shows to be a triumph of automated modules and evolutionary cognitive engineering. Baron-Cohen lays out a series of elegant hypotheses outlining the design features and interrelationships of the modules responsible for these daily triumphs: an eye-direction detector, an intentionality detector, a shared-attention module, and so on. In showing how his proposals account for many dimensions of human social and mental life, he goes far beyond his own penetrating cognitive experiments and neuroscience research. In building his account, he weaves together a seamless tapestry from cognitive science, developmental psychology, primatology, philosophy, cognitive neuroscience, evolutionary biology, anthropology, neurology, behavioral ecology, and literature to create the first natural-science account of the mental machinery that implements the language of the eyes. It is exactly this focus on integrating—within a framework that simultaneously reconciles cognitive, evolutionary, and neural levels of explanation—research from so many disciplines that we suspect will be the most salient characteristic of 21st-century psychology.

If we have eye-direction detectors and companion modules that define and speak the language of the eyes, what do they talk to? Normal humans everywhere not only "paint" their world with color, they also "paint" beliefs, intentions, feelings, hopes, desires, and pretenses onto agents in their social world. They do this despite the fact that no human has ever seen a thought, a belief, or an intention. A growing community of cognitive scientists has concluded that humans everywhere interpret the behavior of others in these mentalistic terms because we all come equipped with a "theory of mind" module (ToMM) that is compelled to interpret others this way, with mentalistic terms as its native language. We are "mindreaders" by nature, building interpretations of the mental events of others and feeling our constructions as sharply as the physical objects we touch. Humans evolved this ability because, as members of an intensively social, cooperative, and competitive species, our ancestors' lives depended on how well they could infer what was on one another's minds. Precisely because such an interpretive system does model the world in terms of unobservable entities (thoughts, intentions, beliefs, and desires), it needs to be coupled to confederate modules that can construct a bridge from the observable to the unobservable. Unobservable entities are invisible to association-learning mechanisms, but they are "visible," over the long run, to natural selection. As chance created alternative cognitive designs, this process "selected" those that implemented the best "betting" system. Over innumerable generations, the evolutionary process selected for modules interpenetrating our perceptual systems that could successful isolate, out of the welter of observable phenomena, exactly those outward and visible signs in behavior that reliably signaled inward and invisible mental states. These modules were built to expect, hook onto, and exploit patterns in the observable world that they already know how to recognize, and to use these targeted cues to fill in the blanks in the ToMM's pre-existing models of other people's mental states. By linking observable cues (such as direction of gaze) to representations of unobservable mental states (such as wants and beliefs), they create what one can think of as the "psychophysics" of the social world.

Yet even well-designed machinery can break down. When the machinery is fundamental to the operation of our minds, the results can be tragic—and deeply illuminating for the cognitive scientist. Breakdowns of specific modules result in subtractions from the impaired individual's model of and experience of the world. A color-blind individual loses one dimension of the visual world. A blind individual loses the entire visual world. But someone whose ToMM is impaired is blind to the existence of other minds, while still living in the same physical, spatial, visual, and many-hued world as unimpaired people do. For beings who evolved to live woven into the minds of mothers, fathers, friends, and companions, being blind to the existence of others' minds is a catastrophic loss. Simon Baron-Cohen and his colleagues were the first to propose that an individual with autism was one whose ToMM had been damaged. They persuasively explained how this hypothesis accounted for the bizarre constellation of symptoms autistics manifest. By considering what companion mechanisms the ToMM needed to function, Baron-Cohen and his colleagues could detect and experimentally track its computational links to what he has termed the eye-direction detector (EDD), the shared-attention mechanism (SAM), and the intentionality detector (ID). As the capstone of this research program, he and his colleagues used these new cognitive models to develop a method for detecting autism far earlier than anyone believed possible and successfully tested it on a base population of 16,000 children.

This sequence of discoveries is one of the key achievements of modern cognitive science. It deserves the careful attention of everyone studying social cognition and development, and because it encapsulates so many of the themes of psychology's metamorphosis it will become recognized as a milestone in the naturalization of the psychological sciences.

John Tooby
Leda Cosmides

Preface

This is a complicated book to write, as I have in mind readers from quite different backgrounds. First, I am writing for my colleagues in the biological and cognitive sciences, whom I hope will find the theory I advance here of sufficient interest that they will respond to the ideas and take them further than I have managed to. Second, I am writing for students in psychology (and related disciplines), for whom I want to make the topic exciting enough that they decide to stay in the field and make their own contributions. Finally, and not least, I am writing for the general reader who has no background in psychology but who wants to keep in touch with where science is going. Keeping in mind all three types of readers on each and every page requires a fair degree of acrobatics, I find. At times I have despaired that this juggling exercise cannot be done. I apologize if I occasionally lapse in this endeavor.

Acknowledgements

This book marks a 15-year voyage for me. When the voyage started, in 1979, I was studying Human Sciences at Oxford, where I was able to combine the study of developmental psychology with evolutionary biology. Among my inspiring teachers there, in these areas, were Peter Bryant, Richard Dawkins, and Tony Boyce. This powerful cocktail of minds enabled me to forge interesting links. The resulting hybrid finds expression in this book: a case study in evolutionary psychology.

I want to take this opportunity to acknowledge the help of many people. I will begin with Uta Frith and Alan Leslie, who supervised my doctoral research at the MRC Cognitive Development Unit in 1982–1985, and June Felton, director of the Family Tree Autistic Unit, with whom I worked for a memorable year as a teacher in 1981–82. These three people fired my interest and helped shape my doctorate thesis (from which much of this book stems).

During the subsequent voyage I have had the good fortune to work with many excellent colleagues: Gillian Baird, Dare Baldwin, Ruth Campbell, Tony Cox, Auriol Drew, Juan Carlos Gòmez, Julie Hadwin, Pat Howlin, Annette Karmiloff-Smith, Sue Leekam, John Moriarty, Natasha Nightingale, Dave Perrett, Howard Ring, Mike Rutter, Marian Sigman, Valerie Stone, Luca Surian, John Swettenham, Heather Van der Lely, and Jane Walker. Much of the research we have carried out together surfaces in this book.

Other colleagues and friends have also critically discussed my ideas with me, and I have appreciated this intellectual exchange enormously. They are Janet Astington, Patrick Bolton, Leslie Brothers, Donald Cohen, Helena Cronin, Peter Fonagy,

Alison Gopnik, Paul Harris, Ami Klin, Franky Happé, Chris Moore, Josef Perner, Angel Riviere, Jim Russell, Amitta Shah, Helen Tager-Flusberg, Digby Tantam, Henry Wellman, Andy Whiten, and Lorna Wing.

In recent years I have also been surrounded by a talented group of doctoral and master's students, who have taught me a lot: Tony Charman, Emma Citron, Pippa Cross, Mary Crowson, Frances Goodhart, Sarah Holroyd, Wendy Phillips, Fiona Scott, and Ruth Staunton. I am pleased to be able to refer to their interesting studies in this book.

I would also like to express my warm thanks to the pupils and teachers at the following schools for children with autism and developmental delay, who have provided essential research facilities and taken part in much of this work: The Sybil Elgar School, Ealing; Radlett Lodge School, Hertfordshire; Griffin Manor School, Plumstead; and Rosemary School, Islington, London.

My work has been funded by the Medical Research Council, the Mental Health Foundation, the Psychiatry Research Trust, the British Council, the Nuffield Foundation, and the Royal Society. In addition, the staff at the National Autistic Society have been continuously helpful in the research.

Alison Gopnik, Juan Carlos Gòmez, Nick Humphrey, and Paul Bethge went way beyond the call of academic duty in reading the first draft of this book, and their careful commentaries undoubtedly helped to improve the final text. I am extremely grateful to them. Teri Mendelsohn and her colleagues at The MIT Press provided excellent editorial advice.

Finally, I want to thank my family, Bridget, Sam, and Kate, for their wonderful support as well as their patience while this was being written in Lolek Holzer's retreat down in Diddywell; Dan, Ash, and Liz, for their fine humor; and my parents and my sister Suzanna, whose influences run deep.

On the Term "Mindblindness"

I first coined the term "mindblindness" to describe autism in an article entitled "Autism: A specific cognitive disorder of mind-blindess" (*International Review of Psychiatry* 2 (1990): 79–88). This paper has also appeared as "Autismo: una alteracao cognitiva especifica de 'cegueira mental'" (*Revista Portuguesa de Pedagogia* 24 (1990): 407–430), as "Autismo: un trastorno cognitivo espicifi-co de 'cuguera de la mente'" (in *El Autismo 50 anos despues de Kanner (1943)*, ed. Canal Bedia (Salamanca: Amaru), and as "Autisme: un trouble cognitif specifique, la 'cecite mentale'" (*Approche Neuropsychologique des Apprentissages chez l'enfant* 5 (1993): 146–154). Nicholas Humphrey (1993) and others use it differently.

Mindblindness

Chapter 1

Mindblindness and Mindreading

Imagine what your world would be like if you were aware of physical things but were blind to the existence of mental things. I mean, of course, blind to things like thoughts, beliefs, knowledge, desires, and intentions, which for most of us self-evidently underlie behavior. Stretch your imagination to consider what sense you could make of human action (or, for that matter, any animate action whatsoever) if, as for a behaviorist, a mentalistic explanation was forever beyond your limits. This is a hard thought experiment. See if it helps to make it more concrete by considering how we understand even a simple human act:

> John walked into the bedroom, walked around, and walked out.

To make sense of this, we ask ourselves why John behaved in this way. A mindreader might answer this question by saying something like this:

> Maybe John was **looking** for something he **wanted** to find, and he **thought** it was in the bedroom.

Or the mindreader might think:

> Maybe John **heard** something in the bedroom, and **wanted to know** what had made the noise.

Or:

> Maybe John **forgot** where he was going: maybe he really **intended** to go downstairs.

A mindreader can generate a longish list of such "maybes" to explain John's behavior—and it is a safe bet that most of them will be based on John's mental states. (In the examples above, the mental-state words are printed in boldface to make it easy to pick them out.)

Now, you and I are mindreaders. I don't mean that we have any special telepathy (see Whiten 1991); I just mean that we have the capacity to imagine or represent states of mind that we or others might hold. Mindreading is nothing mysterious; however, as I hope to show in this book, it is impressive.

Notice that in the above examples our way of thinking about mental states is prefixed by "maybe." We are never 100 percent sure what we or others are thinking (since mental states are to some extent hidden from view), but we nevertheless find it easy to imagine what others may be thinking.

What sense does a person with mindblindness make of John's behavior in the example above? In trying to answer this, we must of course refrain from using any mental-state terms in the explanation. Here is an attempt:

> Maybe John just does this every day, at this time: he just walks into the bedroom, walks around, and walks out again.

Notice that this is not an explanation in terms of any causal motive or reason. Rather, it is simply a statement about possible temporal regularities. It is also very likely to be wrong. When our mindblind person discovers that John does not do this every day at this particular time, he or she will need to come up with another non-mentalistic attempt to explain John's action.

The problem is that there just aren't many simple, readily available, plausible, non-mentalistic explanations for John's behavior. (Try generating some yourself if you don't believe me.) To a person with mindblindness, even this very basic sequence of acts—walking into the bedroom, walking around, and then walking out again—is a real mystery. Now imagine what sense a mindblind person would make of an infinitely more complex social situation (one I observed in my local park in Islington):

Joe and Tim watched the children in the playground. Without saying a word, Joe nudged Tim and looked across at the little girl playing in the sandpit. Then he looked back at Tim and smiled. Tim nodded, and the two of them started off toward the girl in the sandpit.

Again, as mindreaders, we make sense of the situation in mentalistic terms right from the start. For example, we might come up with a rather sinister reading of the situation:

Maybe Joe and Tim had a **plan** to do something nasty to one of the children. Joe **wanted** Tim to **know** that their victim was to be the little girl in the sandpit, and he **indicated** this by the direction of his gaze. Tim **recognized** Joe's **intention** and nodded to tell Joe he had **understood** the **plan**. Then they went over to the little girl, who was **unaware** of what was about to happen.

Or we might come up with a more rosy reading of the situation:

Maybe Joe **wanted** to point out to Tim who it would be fun to play with. Tim **agreed** with Joe's **idea**, so they went over to ask the little girl in the sandpit if she **wanted** to play.

Note that both of these interpretations are littered with mental-state concepts and with terms that express these concepts. (Just look at the bold type.) Indeed, it is hard for us to make sense of behavior in any other way than via the mentalistic (or "intentional"[1]) framework. We just can't help doing it this way; as Fodor (1983) emphasizes, it is a consequence of our biology.

When someone points out all this mindreading to you, it hits you with some force. Recall the apocryphal man who was shocked to discover he had been speaking in prose all his life. We mindread all the time, effortlessly, automatically, and mostly unconsciously. That is, we are often not even aware we are doing it—until we stop to examine the words and concepts that we are using.

What sense would a person with mindblindness make of Joe and Tim in the scene described above? Precious little, is my guess. Why were Tim and Joe smiling at each other? And what did those glances mean? Why did they move off together in the direction of the little girl?

Without a mentalistic framework—or, as Dennett (1987) calls it, the Intentional Stance—a person with mindblindness is thrown back on temporal-regularity accounts or on routine-script explanations (like the one I came up with for why John walked into the bedroom) or is forced to use unwieldy things resembling the "reinforcement-schedule" explanations that behaviorist psychologists construct. None of these seem very useful here. The first two are too limited in their application to the constantly changing social world; the third takes too long to compute. In the heat of a social situation, it pays to be able to come up with a sensible interpretation of the causes of actions quickly if one is to survive to socialize for another day. Non-mentalistic explanations are just not up to the job of making sense of and predicting behavior rapidly. Instead, a person with mindblindness is left confused: Just what are Joe and Tim up to? In the meantime, the mindreader sizes up the situation instantly.

It is probably impossible to imagine what it is like to be mind-blind, in the same way as it is impossible to imagine what it is to be a bat (Nagel 1974).[2] To live in a bat's world, in which objects are known by echo location, must impart a notion of objects so radically different from the notion that we obtain through vision that it may be beyond our imagination. Conversely, it is proba-bly impossible for a mindblind person to imagine what it is like to be a mindreader. In the words of Sperber (1993), "attribution of mental states is to humans as echolocation is to the bat." It is our natural way of understanding the social environment.

The gulf between mindreaders and the mindblind must be vast. Gopnik (1993) gives a vivid account of her attempt to imag-ine just what the world must look like through the eyes of some-one who is mindblind:

> This is what it's like to sit round the dinner table. At the top
> of my field of vision is a blurry edge of nose, in front are

waving hands. . . . Around me bags of skin are draped over chairs, and stuffed into pieces of cloth, they shift and protrude in unexpected ways. . . . Two dark spots near the top of them swivel restlessly back and forth. A hole beneath the spots fills with food and from it comes a stream of noises. Imagine that the noisy skin-bags suddenly moved toward you, and their noises grew loud, and you had no idea why, no way of explaining them or predicting what they would do next.

Tragically, mindblindness is not an idle thought experiment or a piece of science fiction. For some people, it is very real. Gopnik hints at how terrifying it would be to be mindblind. I think she must be right—I certainly would not want to be without the ability to read behavior in terms of mental states. In this book I will discuss the idea that children and adults with the biological condition of autism suffer, to varying degrees, from mindblindess.[3] For reasons to be explored, they fail to develop the capacity to mindread in the normal way.

I intend in this book to extend the ideas first proposed by Nicholas Humphrey in a series of groundbreaking essays published in the 1970s and the 1980s and collected in Humphrey 1984. Humphrey had the brilliant insight that the best way to characterize humans is as *Homo psychologicus*. As he put it (Humphrey 1984, p. 3), "Human beings are born psychologists." He elaborated this as follows:

The ability to do psychology, however much it may nowadays be an ability possessed by every ordinary man and woman, is by no means an ordinary ability. . . . The fact is that, whatever may be the logical problems of describing inner experience, human beings everywhere openly attempt it. There is, so far as I know, no language in the world which does not have what is deemed to be an appropriate vocabulary for talking about the objects of reflexive consciousness, and there are no people in the world who do not quickly learn to make free use of this vocabulary. Indeed, far from being something which baffles human understanding, the open discussion of one's inner experience is literally child's play to a human being, something which children begin to learn before they are more than two or three years old. And the fact that this common-sense vocabulary is acquired so easily suggests that this form of description is natural to human beings precisely because it maps directly onto an inner reality which each invidual, of himself, innately knows. (ibid., pp. 5, 8)

Humphrey's argument, then, is that the ability to see behavior in terms of an agent's mental states is inborn and is the result of a long evolution. Consequently, Humphrey concludes that at one point in our evolution there must have been a time when we lacked this ability. Here is the "Just So" story in which he first proposed this idea:

> . . . once upon a time there were animals ancestral to man who were not conscious. That is not to say that these animals lacked brains. They were no doubt percipient, intelligent, complexly motivated creatures, whose internal control mechanisms were in many respects the equals of our own. But it is to say that they had no way of looking in upon the mechanism. They had clever brains, but blank minds. Their brains would receive and process information from their sense-organs without their minds being conscious of any accompanying sensation, their brains would be moved by, say, hunger or fear without their minds being conscious of any accompanying emotion, their brains would undertake voluntary actions without their minds being conscious of any accompanying volition. . . . And so these ancestral animals went about their lives, deeply ignorant of an inner explanation for their own behavior. (ibid., pp. 48–49)

In calling this a "Just So" story I do not intend to belittle Humphrey's major contribution. It is his own description of his work. He did not attempt to prove the idea scientifically (indeed, there is a real question as to whether such evolutionary claims can ever be proven), so this is just about as far as he took this momentous idea. He of course added some speculations of his own, such as the idea that we mindread by using our own experience of introspection as a simulation of another's mental states—an idea that has been discussed by subsequent "simulation theorists."[4] But aside from these speculations, Humphrey has left it to others to take up his key idea and develop it scientifically.

I hope my own work will contribute to this enterprise. In this book I try to extend Humphrey's idea by presenting a model of the psychological development of mindreading, proposing some fundamental mechanisms that I think must underlie this remarkable ability. I then explore the evidence that children with autism fail to develop this capacity. Next I consider how this might throw light on the evolutionary and neurobiological bases of this capacity. I also argue that the study of autism highlights the role played by two mechanisms that allow us to understand the "language of the eyes."

Chapter 2

Evolutionary Psychology and Social Chess

The approach I take in this book can in part be summed up as an attempt to contribute to the study of evolutionary psychology. Cosmides, Tooby, and Barlow (1992, p. 7) define this as "psychology informed by the fact that the inherited architecture of the human mind is the product of the evolutionary process."

What Is Evolutionary Psychology?

"Evolutionary psychology," of course, strikes a chord with "evolutionary biology," which has transformed the science of biology. As Cosmides et al. suggest, the time is now ripe for psychology to be integrated with biology via evolutionary theory. Every branch of biology, from biochemistry and genetics to zoology and ecology, has been incorporated into a Darwinian framework, and it is something of an embarrassment that psychology has dawdled so far behind in this. One thing I am trying to do here is make up for this by sprinting forward to link arms with psychology's neighbor disciplines in biology.

I do not mean to suggest that all of psychology will be amenable to the Darwinian framework, since it is clear that there will always be a slice of human behavior that has nothing to do with natural selection. (Consider, for example, fashion in clothing.) But wherever psychologists are investigating human universals—the universal aspects of language, color vision, parenting, or (as I argue) mindreading, to name just a few—there is the strong likelihood that the phenomena are biological, innate, and products of natural selection.

A word of qualification is needed about the use of the word "universal." If something is universal, it does not mean that there is no variation in the phenomenon across individuals. On the contrary, it is highly likely that there will be variation, just as there is considerable variation in the size of human stomachs. The point is that every human body *has* a stomach! It is in this sense that I will be arguing that mindreading is universal. Of course a genetic pathology might result in the birth of an individual without a stomach, but such a genetic aberration would not undermine the notion that the stomach is universal; indeed it might help us identify the genes that control the building of the normal stomach. Paradoxically, the genetic pathology that caused a body to be built without a stomach would be further evidence for the evolution of the stomach.

A qualification about the use of the word "biological" is also needed. When I say that a psychological state is biological, I mean that there is a specific process in the brain that controls it. In a sense, all psychological states are biological—"no brain, no mind," goes an old adage. Here I am trying to highlight those psychological states (e.g., talking) that are inevitably universal, in contrast to those (e.g., watching television) that might be universal but are not inevitably so. The former are more like biological instincts—hence Pinker's (1994) use of the phrase "the language instinct." In this book, I will be concerned with what might be thought of as "the mindreading instinct."

Steven Pinker has fruitfully adopted the evolutionary approach to language, using exactly the logic mentioned earlier: try finding a human society in which the people have no language. Such societies are nonexistent, Pinker argues, precisely because language is part of human biology. Cultural variation, of course, is massively evident among the world's 6000 or so languages, but the basic drive to develop and use language—the language capacity—is universal. (Pinker, following Noam Chomsky, also summarizes the evidence for syntactic universals.)

Similarly, the evolutionary approach to parenting is a central part of Bowlby's (1969) "attachment theory."[1] It is clear that human infants (like the immature members of a long line of ancestor species) have a strong drive to "attach" to an adult caregiver, and this is highly adaptive both in terms of the infant's physical survival and in terms of its psychological well-being. Regarding the study of color vision, the very idea of using animal models to investigate human color vision presupposes an evolutionary commitment, and has been remarkably fruitful (Zeki 1993). In this book, following in Humphrey's footsteps, I make the case for the evolution of a mindreading capacity, basing it in part on the evidence of a genetic pathology that causes certain individuals to be born mindblind.

Evolutionary psychology looks at the brain (and thus the mind) as an organ that, via natural selection, has evolved specific mechanisms to solve particular adaptive problems. Darwin (1872) began this approach to psychology. As the examples in the previous paragraphs suggest, how to transmit information between individuals is likely to have been one of the adaptive problem that faced early hominids, and a language center in the brain is a solution to this problem. How to distinguish objects of identical shape and size (e.g., poisonous versus edible berries) is likely to have been another problem facing our evolutionary ancestors; a color-vision center in the brain is an efficient solution to this problem. Similarly, an attachment system solves the adaptive problem of ensuring that immature members of the species survive. Cosmides et al. (1992) use the metaphor of the brain as a Swiss Army knife to make this point. Each blade of the Swiss Army knife was, clearly, designed for a specific purpose: the corkscrew for pulling corks, the screwdriver for driving screws, the scissors for cutting thin materials, the saw for sawing thicker materials, and so on. It makes no sense to try to use the corkscrew to drive screws, or the screwdriver to pull corks, if the knife has a different "mechanism" for solving each of these problems. So it is with the brain, say Cosmides et al. We do not use our color-vision system to talk, or our language system to see color. We use specialized modules for the functions they evolved to solve.[2]

Evolutionary psychology, then, aims to account for the functioning of specific cognitive mechanisms and processes in humans. It also aims to account for the neurobiology, the adaptive value, the phylogenesis, and the ontogenesis of these mechanisms. Finally, it aims to describe any pathologies of these mechanisms. It is worth keeping our sights squarely on this goal. (Most psychological theorists would probably wish to be this broad-ranging, but it is often only those theories that are cast in the evolutionary framework that succeed in keeping their focus on all these separate levels.)

A final qualification about the use of the term "biological": It does not follow that only universals are biological. Individual differences can be biological, too. (Classical Darwinian theory depends on individual differences as something for natural selection to work on.) Similarly, just because something is biological, it does not follow that it is innate. And just because something is innate, it does not follow that it has a modular structure. Finally, even if something is innate and modular, whether it was caused by natural selection is still an open question. (For example, Pinker [1994] clearly disagrees with Chomsky's view that language is innate and modular but not necessarily the product of natural selection.) Claims that various behaviors have innate, biological, modular bases are separable and need independent justification.

In this book, I try to approach the goal of evolutionary psychology with regard to one specific adaptive problem: the rapid comprehension and prediction of another organism's behavior. I aim to sketch how mindreading may be the solution to this problem, and how mindreading has an innate, biological, modular basis. Cosmides et al. (1992, p. 8) define an adaptive problem as a "problem whose solution can affect reproduction, however distally,"[3] since the mechanism that shapes the evolution of a biological system is the system's contribution to the individual's success at reproducing (which enables transmission of the genes that built the biological system in the first place). This, of course, is the familiar concept of natural selection. It is evident, I think, that if another organism's next action is going to be to attack you, or to share its food with you, or to mate with you, you would do well to anticipate this quickly, since any of these actions could indeed "affect reproduction, however distally."

To summarize: One key aim of evolutionary psychology is to describe the evolution of neurocognitive mechanisms. To do this requires the theorist to have some notion of what biologists such as Bowlby (1969) call the *environment of evolutionary adaptedness* (EEA). This is the environment to which the mechanism was an adaptation. In the case of the evolutionary psychology of mindreading, what might have been the relevant EEA?

The Social Environment of Evolutionary Adaptedness

Clearly, the period of recent human history is not the relevant EEA. Cosmides et al. (1992, p. 5) remind us that nothing about our biology—not even our mindreading capacity—is likely to be an adaptation to modern human history. This period is only about 10,000 years old (if one dates it from the advent of agriculture, for example). In contrast, the period relevant to human evolution can be seen as spanning two phases: the Pleistocene epoch (roughly the last 2 million years, during which humans lived as hunter-gatherers), and the several hundred million years before that (during which they lived as foragers of one kind or another). These time spans are important to keep in mind because "they establish which set of environments and conditions defined the adaptive problems the mind was shaped to cope with: Pleistocene conditions, rather than modern conditions" (ibid., p. 5).[4]

That there was massive neurocognitive evolution during the Pleistocene epoch is beyond any doubt. The brain has increased threefold in size in the 3 million years since *Australopithecus afarensis* evolved, going from around 400 cubic centimeters to it current size of about 1350 cubic centimeters (figure 2.1).

The increase in brain size is likely to have had many causes, but one key factor upon which many theorists (Humphrey 1984; Byrne and Whiten 1988; Cosmides 1989; Brothers 1990) agree is the need for greater 'social intelligence'—shorthand for the ability to process information about the behavior of others and to react adaptively to their behavior. It is likely that there was a need for greater social intelligence because the vast majority of

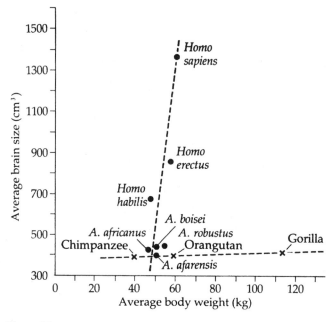

Figure 2.1
Changes in brain size over the last 3 million years. Reproduced from Lewin 1992.

non-human primate species are social animals, living in groups that range from as few as two individuals to as many as 200.

If you are living in a social group of two, the complexities of behavior that you need to make sense of are at least as demanding as our initial example ("John walked into the bedroom"). If you are living in a group of 200, making sense of the social behavior is staggeringly complex. One needs a powerful device—or set of devices—to make sense of actions, rapidly, in order to survive and prosper.

Though we cannot be sure what the EEA for social intelligence was, the striking variety of social organizations in existing non-human primates is a clue. Some primates (e.g., the gibbon) are monogamous. Some (e.g., the gorilla) live in what is called "unimale polygyny," where a single male has control over a group of females and their offspring. Others (e.g., the chimpanzee) live in "multimale polygyny," where several males cooperate to defend a group of widely distributed females and their offspring. Finally, some (e.g., the orangutan) live in what Lewin (1992) calls "exploded unimale polygyny," where a single male defends a group of females and their offspring but the females do not live as a group and instead are distributed over a wide area. If we assume that all these primates evolved from common ancestors, it is plausible that increasing social complexity was an adaptive problem facing them. It may have been as a result of changes in the brain that the complexity of social organization increased, or perhaps new brain mechanisms dedicated to social intelligence evolved to solve the problems posed by the increasing complexities of social behavior. Either way, we are led to look closely at the brain basis for social intelligence (Dunbar 1993).

But let us leave the brain for later and return to the question of social behavior and the EEA. Again, primates are instructive. As the various models suggest, primates live in social environments that are much more complex than the social environments of other animals that live in groups of comparable size, such as the antelope, the sheep, and the cow. (Have you ever noticed how rarely sheep interact?) The difference in complexity lies in the nature of the social interactions. As Lewin (1992, p. 46) puts it: "The [primate] group is . . . the center of intense social interaction that has little apparent direct bearing on the practicalities of life: in the human sphere we would call it socializing, the making and breaking of friendship and alliances."

The challenge for the primate was (and remains) to understand, predict and manipulate the behavior of others in the group. Byrne and Whiten (1988) depict this as the Machiavellian nature of social interaction: to interact in order to use others for various purposes. In primate groups it is this social intelligence that determines who wins higher status. Consider Lewin again on this point:

When you observe other mammal species and see instances of conflict between two individuals, it is usually easy to predict which one will triumph: the larger one, or the one with the bigger canines or bigger antlers, or whatever is the appropriate weapon for combat. Not so in monkeys and apes. Individuals spend a lot of time establishing networks of "friendships," and observing the alliances of others. As a result, a physically inferior individual can triumph over a stronger individual, provided the challenge is timed so that friends are at hand to help the challenger while the victim's allies are absent. (Lewin 1992, p. 129)

The paleontologist Richard Leakey, writing with Lewin, reaches a similar conclusion:

The world of higher primates—of monkeys, apes, and humans—is quintessentially a game of social chess, a keen intellectual challenge. The challenge is keener yet than the ancient board game itself, because the pieces not only unpredictably change identity—knights becoming bishops, pawns becoming castles, and so on—they occasionally switch colors to become the enemy. . . .

What each individual seeks, of course, is reproductive success: producing as many healthy, socially adept off-spring as possible. In birds of paradise, the greatest repro-ductive success (in males) goes to those with the most elaborate plumage and winning display. In red deer, the greatest reproductive success (again, in males), goes to those with the biggest, strongest bodies with which to over-throw rivals, sometimes literally. In higher primates, the greatest reproductive success (in both males and females) is shaped much more by social skills than by physical dis-plays, either of strength or appearance. The complex inter-actions of the primate social nexus serve as an exquisite sorting system, in which the individuals with an edge in making alliances and monitoring the alliances of others may score significantly in reproductive success. (Leakey and Lewin 1992, pp. 191–293)

So, one view is that the evolution of primates is characterized by an increase in the complexity of social interaction, requiring (on the cognitive level) an increase in rapid and adaptive social intelligence and (on the biological level) an increase in different brain mechanisms to support this. The "Machiavellian hypothesis" of brain evolution is by no means proven, since alternative hypotheses are not ruled out by current evidence; it seems a strong contender, however.

Social Chess

The metaphor of "social chess" was Humphrey's. His idea was that intelligence evolved to enable organisms living in complex social groups to understand and take advantage of community living. In Humphrey's words (1984, p. 19), "the chief role of creative intellect is to hold society together." This proposal assumes a sharp distinction between social intelligence and other kinds of intelligence. Here is Humphrey on this:

> "Social intelligence" required, for a start, the development of certain abstract intellectual skills. If men were to negotiate the maze of social interaction it was essential they should become capable of a special sort of forward planning. They had to become calculating beings, capable of looking ahead to yet unrealized possibilities, of plotting, counter-plotting and pitting their wits against group companions no less subtle than themselves. Never before, in their dealings with the non-social world, the world of sticks and stones, not even in their dealings with the world of living predators and prey, had human beings needed their powers of abstract reasoning which they now needed in their dealings with each other. But now their very survival within the social group depended upon it. . . . The life of social animals is highly problematical. In a complex society, such as those we know exist among higher primates, there are benefits to be gained for each individual member both from preserving the overall structure of the group and at

the same time from exploiting and out-maneuvering others within it. Thus social primates are required by the very nature of the system they create and maintain to be calculating beings; they must be able to calculate the consequences of their own behavior, to calculate the likely behavior of others, to calculate the balance of advantage and loss—and all this in a context where the evidence on which their calculations are based is ephemeral, ambiguous, and likely to change, not least as a consequence of their own actions. In such a situation, "social skill" goes hand in hand with intellect, and here at last the intellectual faculties required are of the highest order. The game of social plot and counter-plot cannot be played merely on the basis of accumulated knowledge, any more than can a game of chess.

Like chess, social interaction is typically a transaction between social partners. One animal may, for instance, wish by his own behavior to change the behavior of another; but since the social animal is himself reactive and intelligent the interaction soon becomes a two-way argument where each "player" must be ready to change his tactics—and maybe his goals—as the game proceeds. Thus, over and above the cognitive skills which are required merely to perceive the current state of play (and they may be considerable), the social gamesman, like the chess-player, must be capable of a special sort of forward planning. Given that each move in the game may call forth several alternative responses from the other player this forward planning will take the form of a decision tree, having its root in the current situation and branches corresponding to the moves considered in looking ahead at different possibilities. It asks for a level of intelligence which is, I submit, unparalleled in any other sphere of living. There may be, of course, strong and weak players—yet, as master or novice, we and most other members of complex primate societies have been in this game since we were babies. (Humphrey 1984, pp. 4, 20–21)

The metaphor of social chess works well on several levels. Like chess, social interaction requires one to have a strategy in order to get gradually closer to one's goal, to keep track of the changing positions of various participants and how these affect one's own position, to figure out what might happen next and anticipate it by reacting accordingly, and to outwit one's opponent. It also reminds us that social interaction can be as challenging in problem-solving terms as is chess: just as it is not self-evident exactly where to place one's pieces so that your opponent's key piece cannot move, it is not self-evident how to predict a person's actions, or how to get what you want from another person, or how influence a number of individuals in a group.

The metaphor of social chess risks distorting the concept of social interaction in some ways, too. First, not all social interaction is competitive in the way that chess is. (Even cooperative social interaction requires considerable mindreading.) Second, for many of us, actually playing chess can be rather laborious—a solution to whatever fix one is in does not just pop into one's head. Indeed, in most chess tournaments there is a time limit, since the computing of a solution can be frustratingly slow. In contrast, for most of us, judgements about action in a social situation and about how to get on in a social group do not typically involve laborious logical reasoning. The way we play social chess seems far more intuitive. We just know what to do, and we can easily surmise the reasons that might lie behind someone's actions.

Expert chess players may feel that they intuitively know what the next best move is, and their skill at chess may be an excellent metaphor for how we routinely make judgements during social interaction. Like the chess expert, we are social experts. Our social reasoning process has become automatic and effortless—possibly as a result of years of daily practice, possibly also because, right from the beginning of life, the human brain is programmed to automatically and effortlessly interpret social behavior in this way, as a result of millions of years of evolution. Perhaps we never go through a stage of finding social interaction an effort to decode. Rather, we are born understanding social chess, or at least we have many of the basic principles that we will need in order to make sense of and take part in the game. We have some key neural mechanisms that allow us to "see" the solution to a social situation intuitively.

Chapter 3

Mindreading: Nature's Choice

> In evolutionary terms it must have been a breakthrough.
> . . . Imagine the biological benefits to the first of our
> ancestors who developed the ability to make realistic
> guesses about the inner life of his rivals; to be able to pic-
> ture what another was thinking about and planning to do
> next; to be able to read the minds of others by reading his
> own. (Humphrey 1984)

Before I describe the specific mechanisms that I think evolved to
enable us to mindread, I have to do one last bit of stage setting.
I want to persuade you that mindreading is simply the best way
to make sense of the actions of others. If I can persuade you of
this, then it will become clearer why evolution may have
favored this solution.[1] It will, I think, be easy to convince you,
since I think that the alternatives to mindreading do not even
come a close second in the competition. I will rely mainly on an
argument of Dennett's (1978a) to make this case.

Here, then, is why mindreading is a wonderful thing for us to
have: Attributing mental states to a complex system (such as a
human being) is by far the easiest way of understanding it. By
understanding, Dennett means coming up with an explanation
of the complex system's behavior and predicting what it will do
next. Dennett calls this ability "adopting the Intentional Stance."
The term "Intentional Stance" refers to our ability to attribute
the full set of intentional states (beliefs, desires, thoughts, intentions, hopes, memories, fears, promises, etc.), not just to the specific mental state of intention.

What Are the Alternatives to Mindreading?

Dennett argued that the two alternatives to adopting the
Intentional Stance are attempting to understand systems in
terms of their physical makeup (the Physical Stance) and
attempting to understand them in terms of their functional
design (the Design Stance).[2] We adopt the Physical Stance to
understand systems whose physical makeup we know about.
For example, we all know a bit about human anatomy. We know
enough to be able to reason that the skin bleeds when it is cut
because blood vessels have been severed. In this instance, our
understanding of the body takes the form of adopting the
Physical Stance—using a "folk biology." However, attempting
to understand the behavior of a person or of any kind of animal
by adopting the Physical Stance would be a non-starter, in view
of the state of our knowledge: we would need to know about the
millions of different physiological (brain) states that give rise to
different behaviors in order to understand animal or human
behavior in purely physical terms.

Mindreading (or adopting the Intentional Stance) is therefore
an infinitely simpler and more powerful solution than adopting
the Physical Stance. Thus, in response to the first example in
chapter 1, the answer

> John went into the bedroom because he **wanted** to find his
> jacket and **thought** it was in there

may be just as accurate as

> John went into the bedroom because six **brain states** (A,
> D, F, H, J, and Q) were activated in a particular sequence
> (D, J, Q, A, F, and H);

however, the former is far simpler to compute. The latter
account assumes that John's current behavior is due to just six
brain states, active in a particular sequence. In reality, of course,
it is likely to be a vastly larger number than this. This Physical
Stance account also assumes that these brain states are known,
which at present they are not. Finally, it assumes that these brain
states are knowable, whereas in reality neither ordinary folk nor

scientists have a "brainoscope" with which to "see" what brain states are active in another person at any given time and then to predict that person's next action.

So much for the first of the alternatives to the Intentional Stance: the Physical Stance is good for some things, but it is not up to the job of predicting the behavior of complex systems. But what of the second alternative? According to Dennett, we adopt the Design Stance when we are ignorant about the physical makeup of a system (the Physical Stance is therefore not available to us) but are trying to understand the system in terms of the functions of its observable parts. For example, I need not know anything about silicon chips or other details of my computer's physical makeup to predict its behavior. Instead, I can refer to some of its design features: the Delete key (whose function is to rub out what I have just typed), the Escape key (whose function is to clear the screen), and so forth. Not only is the Design Stance explanatory (to a degree); it also allows us to predict what the system will do next if this button or that switch is pushed.

The Design Stance works well when we wish to explain a system composed of clearly observable and operational parts, such as an alarm clock, a television, or a thermostat. Note, however, that mindreading would work just as well. Indeed, many people reason about their computers in very mentalistic ways, saying things like

> My computer is displaying this command because it **thinks** I have finished.

Dennett reminds us that this is how we talk about thermostats too:

> It **wants** to keep the room at a constant temperature, and **thinks** that the room is getting too warm.

However, the Design Stance seems just as useful in these cases. For example, we might say

> My computer isn't working because it is not plugged in.

But adopting the Design Stance toward understanding the behavior of people or other animals would not get one very far, since people and animals have very few external, operational parts for which one could work out a functional or design description. It might work well enough for making sense of people's reflexes (e.g., an eye blinks when you blow on its surface or poke it with your finger, because it has a pressure detector on its surface whose function is to close the eye). The Design Stance is also pretty useful for studying unobservable processes; however, it is of little value in making sense of and predicting moment-by-moment changes in a person's behavior.

For Dennett, we use mindreading because it works. It is a pragmatic argument. Dennett is not committed either way on the question of whether there really are such things as mental states inside the heads of organisms. We ascribe these simply because doing so allows us to treat other organisms as rational agents. For Fodor (1983), it is not just a pragmatic issue. We mindread, according to him, because there really are mental states inside our own and other organisms' heads. Inferring these states gives us a powerful lever in making sense of and predicting behavior. (In contrast, the Churchlands [1981] acknowledge that we employ mindreading but argue that the idea that mental states actually exist is patently false.)

Let us just focus on Fodor's view that the solution evolution came up with to enable us to understand and predict our own and other people's behavior—or the behavior of any complex system—is the Intentional Stance, or what we have so far been calling mindreading. As Fodor points out, it is a simple-to-use and powerful theory, which is exactly what we need when we are in the thick of a social situation. It also leaves the alternatives miles behind. Evolution was not going to wait around for human scientists to invent a brainoscope before primates (early hominids included) could understand and participate in complex social interaction. If it had done so, the hominid line would have died out long ago. Instead, I argue, it gave us a far simpler device, something akin to a mindoscope, and it gave it to us as part of our neural anatomy, which allows us to mindread other creatures.[3]

Just to make this more real, imagine that a salesman is stand-
ing at your front door, waiting for you to sign a piece of paper.
You need to reason quickly about his behavior and what he is
likely to do next. Making inferences about his desires, intentions,
thoughts, and motives allows you to do this. Now imagine that
you are an early hominid, and that another early hominid offers
to groom you and your mate. You need to reason quickly about
whether you should let him approach. Again, making inferences
about whether his motives are purely altruistic or whether he
might be deceitful is a reasoning strategy that you can apply in
time to react to a social threat. The modern human, at least,
seems to be extremely quick at mindreading, and appears to
engage in it automatically. My guess is that hominids have been
doing this for a long time.

Mindreading also goes under the name "folk psychology"—
and that may be a better term for it,[4] since it reminds us that it is
simply our everyday way of understanding people. As Dennett
(1987, p. 48) points out,

> We use folk psychology all the time, to explain and predict
> each other's behavior; we attribute beliefs and desires to
> each other with confidence—and quite unselfconsciously—
> and spend a substantial portion of our waking lives formu-
> lating the world—not excluding ourselves—in these terms.
> . . . Every time we venture out on the highway, for exam-
> ple, we stake our lives on the reliability of our general
> expectations about the perceptual beliefs, normal desires
> and decision proclivities of the other motorists. We find . . .
> that it is a theory of great generative power and efficiency.
> For instance, watching a film with a highly original and
> unstereotyped plot, we see the hero smile at the villain and
> we all swiftly and effortlessly arrive at the same complex
> theoretical diagnosis: "Aha!" we conclude (but perhaps not
> consciously), "He wants her to think he doesn't know she
> intends to defraud her brother!"

A final alternative to mindreading is what might be called
"adopting the Contingency Stance." This entails learning or

innately recognizing the behavioral contingencies between another organism's behavior and their effects. For example, seeing a cat arch its back might make you anticipate that it is about to pounce. Seeing a gorilla flare its nostrils, open its eyes and mouth wider, and beat its chest might make you anticipate that it is about to attack. The Contingency Stance is probably a subspecies of the Design Stance. In essence, to adopt this stance is to characterize the organism as a behaviorist—the most obvious alternative to a mindreader. It is highly likely that most non-human organisms adopt this stance in their interactions with other animals, and that we humans often make use of it too. Seeing someone yawn in mid-conversation, you might anticipate that the conversation will be ending very soon; seeing someone raise his fist might act as a powerful cue for you to flinch and take self-protective measures. Darwin's studies suggested that a long line of organisms display, recognize, and react to bodily expressions. However, picking up behavioral cues is obviously useful only if such cues are available. What mindreading allows one to do is predict behavior even in situations where there are no behavioral cues. For example, not having heard from a friend for several months, you might think that she thinks you have offended her in some way; you might then decide to give her a ring to check how things are. The friend's lack of behavior can hardly be considered a specific "cue," but a mindreader can work with only minimal behavioral cues (and even with none whatsoever—one can attribute mental states to an invisible entity, like God).

Mindreading and Communication

So far, in attempting to persuade you that mindreading is a really good thing to have, I have focused on its role in making sense of behavior. However, a second reason why mindreading is useful, and thus why it may have evolved, is the way in which it allows us to make sense of communication. Let me add to my argument about the virtues of mindreading by saying just a little about its role in communication.

A range of theorists—Grice (1967), Sperber and Wilson (1986), Austin (1962)—have argued that when we hear someone say something (or when we read a sentence in a novel), aside from decoding the referent of each word (computing its semantics and syntax), the key thing we do as we search for the meaning of the words is imagine what the speaker's communicative intention might be.[5] That is, we ask ourselves "What does he mean?" Here the word "mean" essentially boils down to "intend me to understand." Put another way, the key question that guides our comprehension process is "Just what is he driving at?" The notion is that not only do we pay attention to the actual words a speaker uses; we also focus on what we think was the gist of what he or she wanted to say or wanted us to understand. Sperber and Wilson (1986) call this a search for "relevance"—the listener assumes that the meaning of an utterance will be relevant to the speaker's current intentions. Thus, when the cop shouts "Drop it!" a robber is not left in a state of acute doubt over the ambiguity of the term "it." Rather, the robber makes a rapid assumption that the cop meant (i.e., intended the robber to understand) that the word "it" should refer to the gun in the robber's hand. And at an even more implicit level, the robber rapidly assumes that the cop intended the robber to recognize his intention to use the word in this way. In decoding figurative speech (such as irony, sarcasm, metaphor, or humor), mindreading is even more essential.

The above analysis of language makes clear that in decoding speech we go way beyond the words we hear or read, to hypothesize about the speaker's mental states. This analysis applies not only to speech but also to non-verbal communication. Thus, when I gesture toward a doorway with an outstretched arm and with an open palm, you immediately assume that I mean (i.e., intend you to understand) that you should go through the door.

A more complex example (from Sperber and Wilson 1986) makes the point of how we search the context in order to infer a speaker's communicative intention even more clearly:

Flag-seller: Would you like to buy a flag for the Royal National Lifeboat Institution?

Passerby: No thanks, I always spend my holidays with my sister in Birmingham.

Sperber and Wilson's analysis of this brief exchange runs as follows:

> To see the relevance of the passerby's response, the hearer must be able to supply something like the premises [below] . . . , and derive something like the contextual implication [below]:
>
> (a) Birmingham is inland.
> (b) The Royal National Lifeboat is a charity.
> (c) Buying a flag is one way of subscribing to a charity.
> (d) Someone who spends his holidays inland has no need of the services of the Royal National Lifeboat Institution.
> (e) Someone who has no need of the services of a charity cannot be expected to subscribe to that charity.
>
> [Therefore,] the passerby cannot be expected to subscribe to the Royal National Lifeboat Institution. (ibid., pp. 121–122)

In some ways, what the passerby said was rather unconnected. Nevertheless, there is still a way we can work out why he might have said it and what he might have wanted to mean: by representing all of the above thought steps that could have been in his mind. Our mindreading fills in the gaps in communication and holds the dialogue together.

Let us take just one other example of this, this one from Pinker (1994, p. 227):

Woman: I'm leaving you.
Man: Who is he?

In order to have produced this phrase, the man must have thought that the woman was leaving him for another man. When we make this attribution to the man, the dialogue hangs together perfectly. If we did not make it, the dialogue would seem disconnected, almost a random string of words. As mindreaders, we perceive the man's sentence as far from random.

Presumably, a person with mindblindness would struggle in vain to find any relevance in this exchange.

The other way in which mindreading is held to play an essential part in successful communication is in the speaker's monitoring the informational needs of the listener—that is, in the speaker's judging what the listener may already know or be ignorant about, and what information he or she should supply so that the listener will be able to understand the message. An utterance like "Shall we?" will not, in most contexts, be enough to get the listener to know what on earth you were intending to say. (A dance hall might be an exception in the case of this particular phrase.) Rather, the speaker computes that, if the listener is to have even a glimmer of an idea of what he is trying to say, he must provide more information—for example, "Shall we go to Devon this weekend?"

Furthermore, for communication to succeed, the speaker must monitor whether the meaning of an utterance has been received and understood as he or she intended it to be, or whether rephrasing is required to resolve ambiguity. Dialogue understood in this way becomes much more than the production of speech: it is revealed as intrinsically linked to the use of mindreading skills. The alternatives to mindreading (such as adopting the Physical or the Design Stance, or using what Sperber and Wilson (1986) call a "code" approach to language) turn out to be inadequate means of making sense of human communication and action. And in terms of the evolutionary "fitness" value of mindreading in communication, it is clear that an ability to go beyond the words heard to the speaker's intention would allow the listener to judge whether the speaker was being deceitful or genuine.

A final sense in which language and mindreading are intimately related rests on the idea that language functions principally as a "printout" of the contents of the mind. We speak to one another to share our ideas, thoughts, and experiences. Whether mindreading came first, and language evolved to facilitate this, or the other way around, remains unclear.

To summarize: Mindreading is good for a number of important things, including social understanding, behavioral prediction, social interaction, and communication. The lack of competitive alternatives to mindreading that could produce equal or better success in these domains makes it clearer why natural selection might have latched onto mindreading as an adaptive solution to the problem of predicting behavior and sharing information. I mean, what other real choice did Nature have?

Chapter 4

Developing Mindreading: The Four Steps

> To be a viable hypothesis about human psychological
> architecture, the design proposed must be able to meet
> both solvability and evolvability criteria: It must be able to
> solve the problems that we observe modern humans rou-
> tinely solving and it must solve all the problems that were
> necessary for humans to survive and reproduce in ances-
> tral environments. (Tooby and Cosmides 1992, p. 110)

In the preceding chapter I suggested that natural selection had
produced a mindreading system. Anthropological data suggest
that talk about mental states crops up in every culture in which
it has been sought—that it is a universal (Brown 1991; Avis and
Harris 1990). In this chapter I will propose four mechanisms that
might underlie the universal human capacity to mindread. I
hope these four mechanisms meet the solvability and evolvabil-
ity criteria of Tooby and Cosmides. I leave it to you to decide if
my proposed mechanisms are satisfactory. Are they up to the
job of solving the puzzle of how we modern humans read
minds? And could they have solved the mindreading problems
that ancient hominids were faced with?

The four mechanisms I will describe can be thought of as four
separate components of the human mindreading system (Baron-
Cohen 1994a,b, 1995c), as illustrated in figure 4.1. As Leslie
(1994) suggests, "[it] should be possible to establish links
between properties of the world [and] processing subsystems
specialized for tracking those properties." These mechanisms
roughly reflect four properties of the world: volition, perception,
shared attention, and epistemic states. They are not intended to
be the only mechanisms (I will address the possibility that there

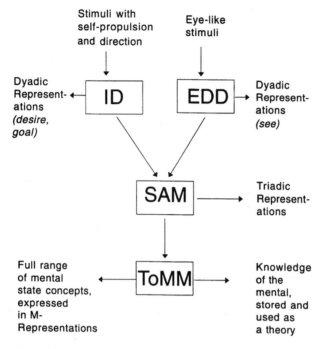

Figure 4.1
The mindreading system.

may be others in chapter 8), but here I will try to make the case that at least these four may be involved in mindreading.

The Intentionality Detector (ID)

The first mechanism that I suggest must be part of the modern human infant's innate endowment for reading mental states in behavior I call the *Intentionality Detector*. (I must apologize to Sigmund Freud, in case he had a copyright on the name. Invoking Freud here also gives you a clue as to how to pronounce it.) In my theory, ID is a perceptual device that interprets motion stimuli in terms of the primitive volitional mental states of goal and desire. I see these as primitive mental states in that they are the basic ones that are needed in order to be able to make sense of the universal movements of all animals: approach and avoidance.

If you see an animal moving, be it an amoeba, a mouse, or a British prime minister, all you need to refer to in order to begin to interpret its movement are these two basic mental states. They allow you to interpret its movement in such terms as

> Her **goal** is to go over there

or

> It **wants** to get the cheese

or

> It **wants** to get away from this

or

> He **wants** power.

Function

How does ID work? The basic idea is that this device is activated whenever there is any perceptual input that might identify something as an agent. The kinds of perceptual input that ID might take include anything that is agent-like. This could be anything with self-propelled motion. Thus, a person, a butterfly, a billiard ball, a cat, a cloud, a hand, or a unicorn would do. Of course, when we discover that the object is not an agent—for example, when we discover that its motion is not self-caused—we can revise our initial reading. The claim, however, is that we readily interpret such data in terms of the object's goal and/or desire.

I suggest that ID is the first basic mechanism human infants need to get into the mindreading game for several reasons. First, the mechanism must be one that can take input via any modality in which it might come (vision, touch, and audition being the principal ones here) and from stimuli which vary hugely in form. The visual input might look as shapeless as an amoeba, as weird as a giraffe or an elephant, or as minimal as a stick insect.

Because of their self-propelled motion, all these are instantly interpretable as agents with goals and desires, despite the great variety of their forms.

So much for having a mechanism that is indifferent to form. What about its amodal property? It may help you to see why ID has to be amodal (or supramodal, perhaps) to imagine a situation in which you have no visual input, only tactile information. You might feel something touch you in the dark, or something gently push you from behind, or something firmly holding your hand and placing it onto an object. (If you were blind, you would have your ID triggered this way continually.) Again, such tactile experiences are instantly interpretable in terms of an agent with a goal of doing something to you.

Now suppose that you are in a situation in which there is no relevant visual or tactile information, only auditory stimuli. Imagine that you are sitting in your living room one dark night, just relaxing. Suddenly you hear a shrill, persistent, screech-like sound. You sit up quickly, thinking "What on earth was that?" Without having seen or felt anything, you will nevertheless in all likelihood readily interpret this as a possible agent—an animal calling, or a person crying out in distress.

ID, then, is really very basic. It works through the senses (vision, touch, and audition), and its value lies in its generality of application: it will interpret almost anything with self-propelled motion, or anything that makes a non-random sound, as a query agent with goals and desires. It is based on Premack's (1990) important idea that goal detection is hard-wired into our species, goals being perceived by a certain kind of motion perception.[1] From the way I have described ID, though, the kind of motion perception that would trigger it is really rather broad.

Mandler (1992) also attempts to specify what distinguishes the motion of an agent from that of something inanimate. The latter is usually seen as the consequence of a force coming from another object, whereas agents, Mandler rightly emphasizes, are self-propelling. Specifying a precise pattern of motion that all agents display is, I think, not necessary when trying to specify the input conditions for ID, since it makes sense that ID should have its parameters set fairly loosely.[2] That way, if anything, it will overattribute agency (and therefore goals and desires) to anything that just might be an agent. This will, of course, lead to some false positives (e.g., interpreting a moving cloud as an agent)—but experience could then let you override the signal "There is an agent," given other types of knowledge. In evolutionary terms, it is better to spot a potential agent, and start checking its desires and goals, than to ignore it. In the game of survival, it is best not to miss a single trick.

This, then, is the first mechanism that I assume the infant needs in order to get into mindreading. It is in some ways similar to the mechanism Leslie (1994) calls ToBy, meaning the infant's Theory of Bodies. However, as Leslie describes it, ToBy's function also encompasses our understanding of physical causality. It is, in his words, a "mechanics module [whose] goal, in general, is to arrive at a description of the world in terms of the mechanical constitution of physical bodies and the events they enter into." In this regard, it is not a mechanism that has evolved specifically to make sense only of the social or the animate world, as ID is.[3] On the other hand, ID is similar to what Leslie calls ToMM$_1$ (Theory of Mind Mechanism, System 1) in that it interprets the actions of agents as goal-directed. ToMM$_1$ in Leslie's scheme is exclusively agent-centered; however, as will become clear in the next subsection, ID can read goal-directedness into the movements of non-agents too. Hence my reason for distinguishing ID.

Evidence

What is the evidence for the existence of ID? Here I limit my argument to pointing to four sources of evidence:

First, Reddy (1991) has shown that very young infants are sensitive to changes in an adult's goal. For example, they respond to the distinction between a give and a tease.[4]

Second, in an early and now-classic study, Heider and Simmel (1944) found that when subjects were asked to watch a silent film in which geometric shapes moved around, and were then asked to describe what they had just seen, they tended to anthropomorphize (or ascribe agency to) the geometric shapes. These subjects used a rich vocabulary of volitional mental-state terms in their accounts, all of which they attributed to the shapes. Figure 4.2 shows a frame from one of these films. Describing this scene, only one of Heider and Simmel's subjects did not ascribe agency and intentionality to the shapes. This odd subject instead described the film (as a whole) almost entirely in geometric terms:

> A large solid triangle is shown entering a rectangle. It enters and comes out of this rectangle, and each time the corner and one-half of one of the sides of the rectangle form an opening. Then another, smaller triangle and a circle appear on the scene. The circle enters the rectangle while the larger triangle is within. The two move about in circular motion and then the circle goes out of the opening and joins the smaller triangle which has been moving around outside the rectangle. Then the smaller triangle and the circle move about together, and when the larger triangle comes out of the rectangle and approaches them, they move rapidly in a circle around the rectangle and disappear. The larger triangle, now alone, moves about the opening of the rectangle and finally goes through the opening to

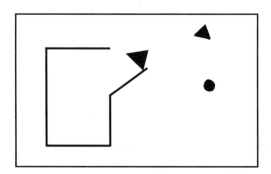

Figure 4.2
A frame from one of Heider and Simmel's films, showing a geometric shape "trying to escape" from a container. Adapted from Heider and Simmel 1944.

the inside. He [*sic*] moves rapidly within and, finding no opening, breaks through the sides and disappears. (ibid., p. 246)

As a narrative this passage is intensely boring. What makes it boring, of course, is precisely the lack of ascription of animacy (with the exception of one instance of the word "He" in the last sentence), and the lack of ascription of intentionality. It is as if this particular subject was mindblind. (Heider and Simmel do not comment on why this subject differed from all the others.) In contrast, here is a typical description, given by one of Heider and Simmel's other subjects, of exactly the same stimulus. Clearly this subject perceived the motion of the shapes in intentional and agentive terms. (I have boldfaced the mental-state terms.)

A man has **planned** to meet a girl, and the girl comes along with another man. The first man **tells** the second to go; the second **tells** the first, and he shakes his head. Then the two men have a fight, and the girl starts to go into the room to get out of the way and **hesitates** and finally goes in. She apparently does not **want** to be with the first man. The first man follows her into the room, after having left the second in a rather weakened condition leaning against the wall outside the room. The girl gets **worried**, and races from one corner to the other in the far part of the room. Man number one, after being rather silent for a while, makes several approaches at her; but she gets to the corner across from the door, just as man number two is **trying** to open it. He evidently got banged around and is still weak from his **efforts** to open the door. The girl gets out of the room in a sudden dash just as man number two gets the door open. The two chase around the outside of the room together, followed by man number one. But they finally **elude** him and get away. The first man comes back and **tries** to open his door, but he is so **blinded** by **rage** and **frustration** that he cannot open it. So he butts it open and in a really mad dash around the room he breaks in first one wall, and then another. (ibid., p. 247)

Now, this narrative is much more exciting! This is purely a function of the ascription of agency and intentionality, both of which are plentiful in this example. I have not highlighted the terms referring to agency, since these are so frequent. Clearly this subject, like virtually all the other subjects in the study, was a mind-reader. The fact that similar results have been obtained with children as viewers (Dasser, Ulbaek, and Premack 1989) suggests that we spontaneously interpret a wide variety of moving shapes as agents driven by mental states. Some recent experiments (Gergely et al., in press) suggest that infants perceive geometric shapes in the same way.

A third clue to the existence of ID comes from David Perrett and his colleagues (Perrett and Mistlin 1990; Hietanen and Perrett 1991), who have identified cells in the temporal lobe of the monkey brain that respond selectively to the sight of another animal facing forward, even if seen in profile.[5] One can think of these as part of ID, detecting the animal's goal (to move forward). Yet other cells fire selectively to tactile stimulation by an agent other than oneself, which suggests that there may be specific neural structures sensitive to another agent having a goal of doing something to the observer.

Fourth, some patients with focal brain damage have been found to lose the specific ability to categorize things as animate or inanimate. This suggests that ID may be localized and dissociable from other parts of the cognitive system (Warrington and Shallice 1984).

The Eye-Direction Detector (EDD)

The second mechanism that I propose the modern human infant possesses as part of its evolutionary endowment I call the *Eye-Direction Detector* (EDD). Whereas the Intentionality Detector works through vision, touch, and audition, EDD works only through vision. As will become apparent, it is a specialized part of the human visual system.[6]

I suggest that in the human case EDD has three basic functions: it detects the presence of eyes or eye-like stimuli,[7] it computes whether eyes are directed toward it or toward something else, and it infers from its own case that if another organism's eyes are directed at something then that organism sees that thing. This last function is important because it allows the infant to attribute a perceptual state to another organism (such as "Mummy sees me"). In this regard, EDD interprets data in terms of a different, primitive mental state than does ID. ID interprets stimuli in terms of the volitional mental states of desire and goal; EDD interprets stimuli in terms of what an agent sees. It can also do a few more things in conjunction with the third mechanism. For the moment, however, let me focus on the functions I have listed so far.

EDD's First Basic Function: Detecting Eyes
It is useful to think in terms of another organism's eyes triggering EDD to fire, much as Tinbergen (1951) described the functioning of an Innate Releasing Mechanism.[8] The idea is that, whenever EDD detects eye-like stimuli, it fixates on these for relatively long bursts and starts to monitor what the eyes do. It then represents the varieties of eye behavior.

We can infer the presence of EDD in the human neonate from the studies by Daphne Maurer and her colleagues (see, e.g., Maurer and Barrera 1981). These workers found that 2-month-old infants looked almost as long at the eyes as at a whole face but looked significantly less at other parts of the face (figure 4.3). This pattern of results was replicated by Haith, Bergman, and Moore (1977) and by Hainline (1978). At the very least, this shows a natural preference for looking at the eyes over looking at other parts of the face.

During breast feeding the infant is of course in a good position to see the mother's eyes. Mothers, quite unconsciously, gaze at their infants for very long durations (more than 30 seconds), and this makes their eyes akin to what Stern (1977) called "supernormal" stimuli. It may be the contrast of the mother's eyes that makes them salient in the face (ibid.). For the infant, then, I assume that the eyes must seem to pop out of the face it is observing. This is probably the case for adults too.

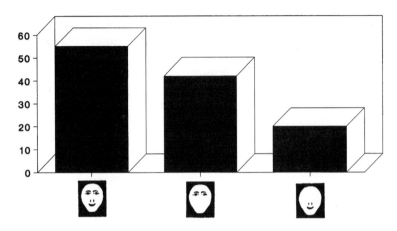

Figure 4.3
Mean length of fixation (seconds) by 2-month-olds shown face-like drawings.
Adapted from Maurer 1985.

EDD's Second Basic Function: Detecting the Direction of Eyes
The second thing EDD does is compute whether the eyes it is
looking at are directed at it or at something else. To do this, EDD
has to represent the relation between the eyes it detects and the
thing toward which the eyes are directed. When another organism's eyes are directed toward the infant's own eyes, EDD
records this. In evolutionary terms, it is clearly highly adaptive
to become aware that another organism has you within its
sights.

What evidence is there that EDD can represent the direction
of eyes it detects? Let me present two sources of evidence.

First, 6-month-olds look 2 to 3 times longer at a face looking
at them than at a face looking away (Papousek and Papousek
1979).[9] In a related vein, one of our recent studies (Baron-Cohen
and Cross 1992) showed that computation of eye direction was
easily within the ability of normal 3-year-olds. The children
were asked which of two photographs of faces was looking at
them. Each pair contained one face looking straight ahead and
one looking away (figure 4.4). In some pairs, only eye direction

Figure 4.4
Two examples of stimuli presented to 3-year-olds, who were asked "Which one is looking at you?" Reproduced from Baron-Cohen and Cross 1992.

was available as a cue, since both faces were facing forward (toward the subject); in other pairs, both nose and eye direction were available. It was apparent that even 3-year-old normal children could make this distinction with either set of cues. Work conducted by Butterworth (1991) and by Vicera and Johnson (1994) suggests that this skill is likely to be present during infancy.

Second, it would seem that whenever EDD detects a pair of eyes that are in mutual contact with its own, this triggers physiological arousal with pleasurable consequences. There is clear evidence of physiological arousal produced by mutual eye contact. For example, galvanic skin responses increase with mutual eye contact (Nichols and Champness 1971), and brain-stem activation has been reported in response to eye stimuli in monkeys (Wada 1961). These measures of arousal might, of course, be indicators of positive or negative emotion. However, in the case of human infants the evidence suggests positive emotion, since eye contact reliably triggers smiling (Wolff 1963; Stern 1977; Schaffer 1977).

Stern (1985) points out that an infant's control over its visual system is precociously mature, enabling the infant to make or break eye contact and thus regulate the degree of eye contact and the amount of physiological arousal that the infant can cope with at a time. Too much might be uncomfortable; too little might be understimulating. Since what constitutes a comfortable level of arousal is likely to vary from one infant to another, it makes good sense that the infant should have its own regulatory mechanism to control this. There is mounting evidence that infants have a drive to maintain an optimal level of stimulation (Maurer 1993). Furthermore, as all parents know, infants and toddlers love to play peekaboo, which is all about occluding the eyes and then revealing them. This innocent little game may be quite important (Bruner 1983), not least because it exercises the infant's EDD.

EDD's Third Basic Function: Interpreting Gaze as "Seeing"
EDD codes mutual eye contact as "Agent sees me" (and "I see

Agent"). This presumes that the infant already knows that eyes can see. I assume that the infant obtains this knowledge from the simple contingencies of closing and opening its own eyes. (Eyes closed produces the experience of not seeing; eyes open produces the experience of seeing.) Furthermore, the infant has experience of its own eyes' moving, which results in a change in the relation between itself and the world. (Now Self sees A; now Self sees B; now Self sees C; etc.) Thus, from very early on, infants presumably distinguish seeing from not-seeing, or seeing-A from seeing-B. Although this knowledge is initially based on the infant's own experience, it could be generalized to an Agent by analogy with the Self. (The possibility that the three basic functions of EDD summarized above may be developmentally ordered suggests that relevant experiments need to be carried out.)

To recap the model so far: We have one mechanism, ID, that reads anything with apparent self-caused motion or apparent self-caused sound in terms of an agent's, goal, and desire. A second mechanism, EDD, is a mindreading mechanism specific to the visual system; it computes whether there are eyes out there and, if so, whether those eyes are "looking at me" or "looking at not-me." Both of these mechanisms are available very early in infancy. This means that we have an infant that, so far, can read behavior in terms of a small set of mental states (goal, desire, and seeing).

Dyadic Representations

ID and EDD can do some useful things, but the kinds of representations they can build are somewhat limited. ID can represent states of affairs like

[Agent-wants-the food]

or

[Agent-has goal-open the door].

EDD can represent states of affairs like

[Agent-sees-me]

or

[Agent-is looking at-the door].

All these representations can be described as dyadic, since they only specify the intentional (i.e., mentalistic) relation between two objects (Agent and Object, or Agent and Self). Though that gets you pretty far, these mechanisms do not allow you to represent that you and someone else (whom we have been calling the Agent) are both attending to the same object or event. And yet that is exactly what one would need in order to be able to communicate about a shared reality and to feel that you and the other person are focusing on and thinking about the same thing.

   Without this crucial next step, your universe would be, in one sense, an "autistic" one. You would have sensations, and you would have images of people doing things and even wanting and seeing things, but you would have no way of knowing that what you and another person were seeing or thinking about was the very same thing. What does one need in order to be aware of a shared universe? What can give you the feeling that you have made contact with someone else's mind, and that someone has made contact with yours?

The Shared-Attention Mechanism (SAM)

Function
Here is where the third mechanism, which I call the *Shared-Attention Mechanism*, comes in. SAM's key function is to build rather interesting things called *triadic representations*. A triadic representation is a representation of a triadic relation,[10] in the same way that a dyadic representation represents a dyadic relation. Essentially, triadic representations specify the relations among an Agent, the Self, and a (third) Object. (The Object can

be another Agent, too.) Included in a triadic representation is an embedded element which specifies that Agent and Self are both attending to the same object. If one wanted to try to express this in symbolic terms, a triadic representation would have something like the following form:

[Agent/Self-Relation-(Self/Agent-Relation-Proposition)].

For example,

[Mummy-sees-(I-see-the bus)]

or

[John-sees-(I-see-the girl)].

This attempt at formalism is useful because it brings out that a triadic representation contains an embedded dyadic representation. However, it may not really capture the complexity of triadic representations; a diagram might do this better. Figure 4.5 is an attempt at a picture of a triadic representation of "You and I see that we are looking at the same object."

SAM builds triadic representations by using any available information about the perceptual state of another person (or ani-

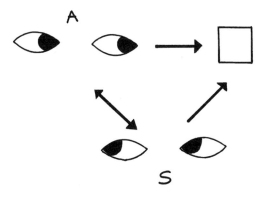

Figure 4.5
A pictorial depiction of a triadic representation. Reproduced from Baron-Cohen 1994b.

mal). In the particular example in figure 4.5, as in the examples expressed symbolically above, SAM has built a triadic representation after receiving information about what another person is looking at. Since this information must have been acquired by monitoring the eye direction of another person, this means that SAM received its information from EDD.

The key thing to emphasize is SAM can build triadic representations, specifying shared attention, only if it receives information about another agent's perceptual state. It then computes shared attention by comparing another agent's perceptual state with the self's current perceptual state. It is like a comparator, fusing dyadic representations about another's perceptual state and dyadic representations about the self's current perceptual state into a triadic representation.[11] Doing this allows SAM to compute that you and I are both seeing the same thing, or smelling the same thing, or touching the same thing, or tasting the same thing, or hearing the same thing. I assume that it is considerably easier for SAM to build triadic representations via EDD, since all this involves is monitoring another person's (or animal's) eye direction toward an object and then checking back once or twice to make sure that you and the other are looking at the same thing. Doing something equivalent via touch, hearing, smell, or taste is possible, but it is not straightforward. For this reason, I propose that there is a privileged relationship between EDD and SAM, although SAM can use information from any modality.

The Relationship between EDD and SAM

So the idea is that SAM needs dyadic representations to build triadic ones, and tends to rely inordinately on EDD because this is the easiest way for it to build triadic representations.[12] To see the force of this argument, consider an example in which two individuals try to verify that they both heard the same noise without making use of vision (and thus of EDD).

David: Did you hear what I just heard?

Jane: What did you just hear?

David: That noise that sounded like a cuckoo.

Jane: I'm not sure if I heard the same thing as you heard.

David: Well, where did the noise you heard come from?

Jane: Over there.

Note that the last line of this conversation involves EDD, since Jane indicates a particular location in space for David to look at. You could try to avoid this by replacing the last line above with "Behind the bushes," but then you would probably get into this kind of sequel:

David: Which bushes?

Jane: The ones over there.

The conversation is thus likely to end up having to involve EDD. My main point here is that, although SAM can build triadic representations via any modality, doing it in the visual one (and specifically using input from EDD) is by far the easiest way.

Consider the limitations of using SAM to verify that you and someone else are touching the same object without using EDD. You would have to touch the object, and then feel the other person's hand touching the same object and touching your hand at the same time—and this could just about be done. Presumably parents of blind children provide this sort of shared attentional experience with their child whenever they want to clarify which object they are communicating about. (This also means that, in their case, SAM must be activated via ID rather than via EDD—see figure 4.1 for clarification.)

The limitations of this use of SAM rapidly become apparent: the only objects that you and the other person could reliably verify you were both attending to would be those that were within reach of both of you. It would make it extremely hard to verify that when communicating about the moon, or about Cousin Steve who lives across the ocean, or about an apple near the top of an apple tree, to name just a few out-of-reach sorts of things, you are actually attending to the same thing. (As for smell or taste, I leave it to you to think of the problems inherent in trying to verify that you and someone else were both smelling the very same smell, or tasting the very same taste, without using EDD.)

Thus, SAM's key function depends heavily on EDD. What is the evidence for this special relationship?

First, gaze monitoring (Scaife and Bruner 1975; Butterworth 1991) is seen in infants from around 9 months of age, and which all children, the world over, show by 14 months or so. In this phenomenon, the infant turns in the same direction that another person is looking at and then shows gaze alternation, checking back and forth a few times to make sure (as it appears) that it and the other person are both looking at the same thing, thus establishing shared visual attention on the same object.

Second, at around the same time, toddlers begin to produce the so-called protodeclarative pointing gesture (Bates et al. 1979)—that is, pointing with an outstretched index finger at an object and then alternating the gaze again, checking back and forth a few times to make sure (as it appears) that the other person has turned to look at the same thing the toddler is looking at. This is a simple but effective way to direct someone else's visual attention to a shared focal object. A toddler also brings objects into another person's line of regard (Lempers et al. 1977).[13]

The Relationship among SAM, ID, and EDD

SAM has a second function: to "talk" to the other two mind-reading mechanisms. We have already seen how SAM depends heavily on talking to EDD. What about its relationship with ID? Here I propose that SAM can make ID's output (e.g., [Agent-has goal-to pick up the rock]) available to EDD. This allows EDD to read eye direction in terms of an agent's goals or desires. This makes a good deal of ecological sense, since agents tend to look at what they want or what they are about to act upon.

In practice this means that when SAM builds a triadic representation via EDD, the relation term in the representation can be visual (e.g., "looks at," "sees," "notices," or "attends to") or it can be filled with one of ID's terms (e.g., "wants" or "has goal").

In addition, one specific use of the goal term that EDD reads is an interesting consequence of EDD's becoming linked up with ID. This is the "goal to pick x out"—i.e., the "goal to refer to x."

What evidence is there that children infer these mental states from eye direction? Regarding evidence for reading the eyes in terms of goal detection, Wendy Phillips, Mike Rutter, and I investigated this with normal infants ranging in age from 9 to 18 months (Phillips, Baron-Cohen, and Rutter 1992). The child was presented with either an ambiguous or an unambiguous action. In one ambiguous action, an adult cupped her hands over the child's hands while the child was engaged in manual activity. In a second ambiguous action, an adult offered an object to the child but withdrew it just as the child began to reach for it. The unambiguous action was simply giving or presenting an object to the child. On most trials, whereas most infants responded to the ambiguous actions by instantly looking at the adult's eyes (within the first 5 seconds after the tease or the block), a small proportion of them did so after the unambiguous action. This suggests that when the goal of an action is uncertain, the first place young children (and indeed adults) look for information to disambiguate the goal is the person's eyes.

In a further study (Baron-Cohen, Campbell, Karmiloff-Smith, et al., in press), it was demonstrated that children use eye direction in the goal-detection function of face processing. When 3–4-year-olds were asked "Which chocolate will Charlie take?" after being shown a display of four chocolates and Charlie's face looking at one of these, they tended to pick the one he was looking at as the goal of his next action (figure 4.6).

Regarding the child's ability to read eye direction in terms of an agent's desires and intended referent, we presented normal 3–4-year-olds with the display of the four chocolates, and placed the cartoon face of Charlie in the center of the display (ibid.). Again, Charlie's eyes were depicted as pointing toward one of the four sweets, randomly selected. In one condition, the subject was asked "Which one does Charlie want?"; in another, "Which one does Charlie say is the (x)?" Children of this age had no difficulty at all in inferring Charlie's desire, or his intended referent,

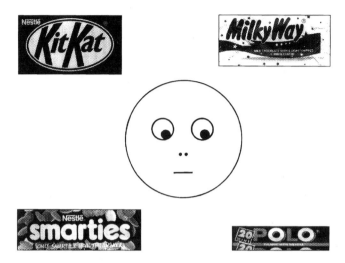

Figure 4.6
The display presented to 3–4-year-olds, who are asked "Which chocolate will
Charlie take?" Reproduced from Baron-Cohen 1994b.

from his eye direction. This was particularly striking, as in a
retest of this experiment the display also included a distracter
cue: a big, bold, black arrow pointing at another of the four
chocolates. Normal 3–4-year-olds appeared to ignore this
"unnatural" cue, and predominantly used the "natural" cue of
eye direction to infer this range of mental states (ibid.).[14]

In summary: There is some evidence that is consistent with
the model according to which, when EDD is linked up to ID via
SAM, eye direction is interpreted in terms of the mental states of
desire, goal, and refer (the latter being a special case of goal).
Baldwin (1991, 1994) and Tomasello (1988) have shown that
even 18-month-olds are sensitive to gaze as a cue to reference.
Though the mental states listed here are simple, they may be
crucial to the subsequent development of the capacity to represent the full range of mental states. One way of thinking about
this change in development is to consider how the first three of
our mindreading mechanisms are related to the fourth: the
Theory-of-Mind Mechanism.

The Theory-of-Mind Mechanism (ToMM)

We need one more mechanism, it seems to me, to complete a sketch of the child's development of mindreading. This is the *Theory-of-Mind Mechanism* (ToMM). This name is taken directly from Alan Leslie's (1994) theory. I am going to go along with much of what Leslie says about the workings of ToMM. However, I need to spell out how ToMM is different from the three other mechanisms, since they are not included in his theory. I also need to make explicit why we need ToMM, over and above the other three mechanisms.

ToMM is a system for inferring the full range of mental states from behavior—that is, for employing a "theory of mind." So far, the other three mechanisms have got us to the point of being able to read behavior in terms of *volitional mental states* (desire and goal) and to read eye direction in terms of *perceptual mental states* (e.g., see). They have also got us to the point of being able to verify that different people can be experiencing these particular mental states about the same object or event (shared attention). But a theory of mind, of course, includes much more.

The first thing that is still needed is a way of representing the set of *epistemic mental states* (which include pretending, thinking, knowing, believing, imagining, dreaming, guessing, and deceiving). The second is a way of tying together all these mental-state concepts (the volitional, the perceptual, and the epistemic) into a coherent understanding of how mental states and actions are related. ToMM does just these things. It has the dual function of representing the set of epistemic mental states and turning all this mentalistic knowledge into a useful theory.

Functions
Regarding ToMM's first function of representing epistemic mental states, Leslie's suggestion (Leslie and Thaiss 1992; Leslie and Roth 1993) is that ToMM processes representations of propositional attitudes of the form

[Agent-Attitude-"Proposition"].

For example,

[John-believes-"it is raining"]

or

[Mary-thinks-"my marble is in the basket"].

Leslie calls these *M-Representations*, and he argues that they are crucial to the ability to represent epistemic mental states. This is because the attitude is directed toward a proposition, and the proposition can be false while the whole M-Representation is true. Thus, to continue the last example, the proposition will be false if in reality my marble is actually in the bucket, but the whole M-Representation can still be true if Mary actually thinks it is in the basket. (That is, what is true is that she thinks it is in there.) This also works well for many other epistemic mental states. So ToMM allows the *referential opacity* that is a key property of epistemic mental states. Referential opacity (or non-substitutability) is the property of suspending the normal truth relations of propositions. An example of this can be found in the Old Testament story of Joseph. The statement

Joseph's brothers **thought** they were bowing down to the prime minister of Egypt

can be true, while

Joseph's brothers **thought** they were bowing down to their brother

may be false, even if the prime minister of Egypt is the same person as Joseph. The second statement will be false if the brothers didn't **know** the prime minister of Egypt was their brother and didn't **recognize** him as their brother. Here the mental-state term **thought** is the "attitude" that the brothers have toward the proposition, and it is the whole M-Representation that must be judged for its truth or falsity, not just the proposition embedded within it.

A second example will serve to clarify this further. The statement

Snow White **thought** the woman selling apples was a kind person

can be true, while

Snow White **thought** her wicked stepmother was a kind person

may be false, even if the woman selling apples is the same person as Snow White's wicked stepmother. The second statement will be false if Snow White did not **know** that the woman selling apples was actually her wicked stepmother.

The fact that normal 4–5-year-olds enjoy and understand these tales of deception suggests that, although the idea of referential opacity is a complex one, we have a facility for understanding it with ease from quite early on in childhood.

Regarding ToMM's second function, that of tying all our mentalistic knowledge together into a coherent whole to make it into a useful theory: We clearly need to do this if we are to use this vital way of interpreting social behavior rapidly and flexibly.

Evidence

What evidence is there for these two functions of ToMM? As before, I point to two sources of evidence for each of the functions.

First, a host of studies show that around the age of 18–24 months human toddlers begin to pretend and recognize the pretending of others, and this seems to mark a qualitative change in their play (Leslie 1987; Dunn and Dale 1984). Leslie argues that the mental state "pretend" is probably one of the first epistemic mental states that young children come to understand.

Second, from 36 to 48 months, children show evidence of understanding additional epistemic states, such as "knowing," and demonstrate that they understand the principle that "seeing leads to knowing" (Pratt and Bryant 1990)—that knowledge is the product of perception. Related to this, a large set of evidence shows that during the same period children come to understand that people sometimes think things that are true (and hence have knowledge, or true beliefs) and sometimes think things that are clearly false (and thus have false beliefs) (Wellman 1990; Perner 1991)—hence their facility at understanding the deception at the heart of "Snow White" and other fairy tales and their growing ability to deceive others (Sodian 1991; Sodian et al. 1992).[15]

Regarding the second function of ToMM: To tie all this mentalistic knowledge into a theory, Wellman (1990) has provided most of the relevant data and argument for why we should call what the young child has a "theory."[16] First, he has shown that children, from the age of 3 years, have an adult-like ontology, dividing the universe into mental and physical entities. Thus, they appreciate that a real biscuit can be seen by several people, can be touched, and can be eaten, whereas a thought-about or dreamed-about biscuit cannot. Related to this, they also understand that dreams and thoughts occur inside the head and are private and not observable to others. Second, Wellman has shown that children use their mentalistic knowledge in highly theory-like ways, reasoning to predict action by following the arrows from left to right in figure 4.7, or explaining action from right to left.

Children probably could also affirm a long list of axioms that constitute the core of their theory of mind, though as yet only a

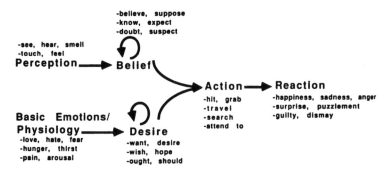

Figure 4.7
A characterization of the human theory of mind. Reproduced from Wellman 1990.

fraction of these have been explicitly stated and tested (such as "seeing leads to knowing," "appearance is not necessarily the same as reality," "people are attracted to things they want," and "people think that things are where they last saw them").

A few words are needed about the phrase "theory of mind," which has come to be shorthand for the capacity to attribute mental states to oneself and to others and to interpret behavior in terms of mental states. It is a phrase that derives from primate research by Premack and Woodruff (1978), who likened the human concept of mind to a theory because mental states are unobservable entities that we use quite successfully to explain and predict behavior. There is some controversy over whether Premack and Woodruff's choice of the word "theory" was really appropriate.[17] It follows from the model I have presented here that I restrict the term "theory of mind" to this relatively late stage of development, when ToMM comes onto the scene.

Relationships among the Four Mindreading Mechanisms

How is ToMM related to the other three mechanisms? Clearly, ToMM must be able to receive inputs from ID and from EDD if it going to be able to integrate the mental states from these two mechanisms into a useful theory. Figure 4.1 shows this happening via SAM. My proposal is that SAM's triadic representations are ideal input to ToMM because their relation slot can also take attitude terms (e.g., desire, attend, goal, refer). My idea is that ToMM is triggered in development by taking triadic representations from SAM and converting them into M-Representations. In its strongest and clearest form, my claim is that without SAM ToMM cannot get started.[18] All these relationships are shown in figure 4.1.

For clarity, I will also divide this model into distinct phases of development. In phase 1 (roughly from birth to 9 months), all the infant has is ID, and the basic functions of EDD, and the only kinds of representations these can build are dyadic. This phase corresponds in part to what Trevarthen (1979) calls "primary intersubjectivity."[19] In phase 2 (roughly from 9 to 18 months),

SAM comes on board. This is something of a qualitative shift, since SAM can build triadic representations that make joint attention possible. And SAM links EDD with ID so as to enable eye direction to be read in terms of the basic mental states. This corresponds roughly to what Trevarthen (1979) calls "secondary subjectivity." Finally, in phase 3 (from about 18 to 48 months), ToMM comes on board, triggered by SAM. ToMM's arrival is heralded by the onset of pretend play. Again, this constitutes something of a qualitative shift for the child, which can now begin to appreciate its own and other people's epistemic states, starting with the mental state 'pretend' and progressing over the next two years to the important mental states of 'knowing' and 'believing'.[20] The child does this by building M-Representations.

In phases 2 and 3, the earlier mechanisms still continue to function (they are in no sense replaced by the new ones). There is, however, a big difference between the other three mechanisms and ToMM, in that the small set of mental states the other three mechanisms can represent possess only two of the properties of Intentionality: aboutness (they are all about things other than themselves) and aspectuality (they can all be about specific aspects of things) (Dennett 1978a; Perner 1991). By contrast, the epistemic attitude concepts processed by ToMM possess a third property of Intentionality: the possibility for misrepresentation (or what was earlier called "referential opacity") (Perner 1991). This was evident in the Snow White story. ToMM, therefore, is both more versatile than the other mechanisms and can represent a larger set of mental-state terms.

Modularity and Mindreading

Some people get very nervous when there is talk about modules. I want to say just a few words about this slippery concept, especially in relation to the mechanisms I have been describing.

Fodor (1983) was perhaps the person who gave the most impetus and the most serious consideration in modern psychology to the notion that the mind and the brain have modular organization, and it was he that made this notion acceptable again after it had been discredited during the nineteenth century's era of phrenology.

Modules, Fodor argued, have

(1) domain specificity,
(2) encapsulation,
(3) obligatory firing,
(4) shallow outputs,
(5) speed,
(6) inaccessibility to consciousness,
(7) a characteristic ontogenetic course,
(8) a dedicated neural architecture, and
(9) a characteristic pattern of breakdown.

As Bates (1993) points out, the first six of these tenets also apply to "overlearning," whereby skills become automatized. It is only the last three tenets that are true of "biological" modules, and even then, it is an open question as to the role of innate and experiential factors in the development of such modules. When these criteria are applied to the systems I have been discussing, some of the mechanisms fit the concept of modularity better than others. For this reason, I have referred to these systems as "neurocognitive mechanisms," rather than as "modules" in the strict Fodorian sense.

The extent to which each of the four mindreading mechanisms is innate or develops as a function of some learning seems to be to be still open to investigation. Clearly, a lot must be prespecified, as I have hinted, though there may be a role for more learning in some of these—especially ToMM. (ToMM seems to differ in kind from the other three components, which, because they use specialized inputs, are more akin to classical modules. The nature of more central modules is still the subject of considerable debate (Leslie 1994; Gopnik and Wellman 1992).)

Before leaving this account of the development of mindreading, I need to justify why I have suggested *four* mechanisms. I have struggled hard to keep the number of mechanisms to the minimum with which to do the job. Clearly, we could have just one big mechanism that does all the things I claim are done by four independent (but connected) mechanisms. My reasons for postulating four distinct modules stem from the evidence from neuropsychology—specifically from the pathologies of autism and blindness, in which these four mechanisms come apart or "fractionate" from one another. I hope to show that there cannot be just one big mechanism. Rather, it appears that Nature can be divided along clear seams, as shown in figure 4.1.

Chapter 5

Autism and Mindblindness

> Imagine a hypothetical being who knows nothing of internal mental states. . . . Such a being might be able to remember, know, and learn, but it would possess no understanding of these activities. The social world, the world of self and others, would be an impoverished place for such a creature. . . . Persons would be seen and heard but there would be no notion of a backlog of ideas and beliefs organizing their actions and personalities. Indeed, for this hypothetical being, no one could be construed as possessing private persona; public present behavior would have no deeper meaning. The concept of a lie would be inconceivable, as would . . . notions such as illusions, beliefs, hunches, mistakes, guesses, or deceptions. It is almost impossible to imagine what such a perspective would be like, how such a creature would view the world. (Wellman 1985, pp. 169–170)

When Henry Wellman wrote these words, he did so having spent many years documenting the evidence for normal children's astonishing competence at mindreading as they develop. For Wellman, the idea of a "hypothetical being" who could not mindread was almost incredible; he proposed the above thought experiment mainly for the purpose of drawing our attention to what life would be like without this remarkable ability.

And remarkable it is. By the end of the first year of life, normal infants, according to the evidence presented in the last chapter, can tell that they and someone else are attending to the same thing, and can read people's actions as directed at goals and as driven by desires. As toddlers, they can pretend and understand pretense. And by the time they begin school, around age 4, they can work out what people might know, think, and believe. According to the model I have outlined, this is due in part to the maturing of four mechanisms that the infant has pre-wired into its brain—its inheritance from a long evolutionary history.

For this model to approach the truth even remotely, each of the four systems should, in principle, be open to damage, the nature of the consequent disability depending on which system is damaged. In this chapter I am going to argue from existing evidence that there are real children—not hypothetical beings—who suffer from mindblindness as a result of damage either to SAM or ToMM. These are children with autism. In contrast, I am going to stress how children with congenital blindness[1] are surprisingly able to mindread, because they have an intact SAM and ToMM despite having no EDD.

A Brief Picture of Autism[2]

Autism is considered the most severe of all the childhood psychiatric conditions. Fortunately, it occurs only rarely, affecting between approximately 4 and 15 children per 10,000. It occurs in every country in which it has been looked for, and across social classes. The key symptoms are that social and communication development are clearly abnormal in the first few years of life, and the child's play is characterized by a lack of the usual flexibility, imagination, and pretense.

The condition may be associated with many biological abnormalities, such as epilepsy, mental handicap, and a variety of brain pathologies. It also appears that in many cases there is a genetic basis to the condition, since the risk of autism or related problems in identical twins or biologically related siblings is substantially higher than would be expected if autism just struck "by chance." At present, autism is unfortunately a lifelong disorder. Thankfully, it sometimes appears to alleviate a little with age, as the child receives the benefits of a range of educational and therapeutic interventions and learns various strategies for adapting to the social world. It is also possible that the improvements with age reflect changes in the underlying pathology, such as might occur if mechanisms began working after a substantial delay rather than being permanently damaged.

The best way to get a sense of what a child with autism is like, if you have never met one, is to read extracts of Kanner's (1943) descriptions of the children in whom he first identified the syndrome:

> He seems almost to draw into his shell and live within himself. . . .

> When taken into a room, he completely disregarded the people and instantly went for objects. . . .

> When a hand was held out to him so that he could not possibly ignore it, he played with it briefly as if it were a detached object. . . .

> He did not respond to being called, and did not look at his mother when she spoke to him. . . .

> He never looked up at people's faces. When he had any dealings with persons at all, he treated them, or rather parts of them, as if they were objects. He would use a hand to lead him. He would, in playing, butt his head against his mother as at other times he did against a pillow. He allowed his boarding mother's hand to dress him, paying not the slightest attention to her. . . .

> . . . on a crowded beach he would walk straight toward his goal irrespective of whether this involved walking over newspapers, hands, feet, or torsos, much to the discomfiture of their owners. His mother was careful to point out that he did not intentionally deviate from his course in order to walk on others, but neither did he make the slightest attempt to avoid them. It was as if he did not distinguish people from things, or at least did not concern himself about the distinction.

Kanner's descriptions pick out the same essential qualities of autism as more recent clinical accounts do, such as those of

Baron-Cohen and Bolton (1993), extracts from which follow:

> . . . he never really seemed to look at anyone directly. Rather, he would look at them only fleetingly or else not at all. Despite this, John seemed to notice everything in minute detail. He could ride his bicycle along the most crowded pavements without knocking anyone over, and he spotted car number plates with a figure four in them long before anyone else had noticed. He would also do things his parents found embarrassing, like grabbing and eating sandwiches from a stranger's plate at restaurants.

> He was very good with his number work and took a great delight in learning multiplication tables. He was also still very quick at jigsaws and could manage even difficult puzzles quite easily: at six years old, he did a 200 piece jigsaw puzzle on his own, and a 100 piece one upside down! Socially, however, he was unable to make any friends whatsoever. He would attempt to join in a game that he liked, but his approaches were so odd that other children tended to ignore him. Most of the time, John was to be found on his own, busying himself with one of his special interests, more absorbed in counting lamp posts than playing with other school children.

> She took great interest in the smell of everything, sniffing food, toys, clothes and (to her parents' embarrassment) people. She even tried to smell strangers in the street. She also liked the touch and feel of things—especially sandpaper. In fact, she insisted on carrying around a small piece of sandpaper in her pocket. Strangely though, she took no interest in the cuddly toys she was given. Lucy's desire to touch and feel things was also a source of embarrassment to her parents. She often tried to stroke stockings on women's legs, even if they were complete strangers. If they tried to stop her, she would have a tantrum.

The key features of the social abnormalities in autism that these descriptions pick out include lack of normal eye contact, lack of normal social awareness or appropriate social behavior, "alone-ness," one-sidedness in interaction, and inability to join a social group.

In 1985, Uta Frith, Alan Leslie, and I proposed that three of the cardinal symptoms in autism—the abnormalities in social development, in communication development, and in pretend play—might be the results of a failure in the development of mindreading. In this chapter I examine this claim with respect to the model I proposed in chapter 4. What is the evidence that children with autism are mindblind?[3] And what is the evidence for the functioning or malfunctioning of each of the four mechanisms in these children?

Autism and ID

Since ID was the first of the primitive mechanisms postulated for normal development, I begin with an examination of how it functions in autism. Recall that ID essentially interprets stimuli in terms of goals and desires—the volitional mental states. Can children with autism understand volitional mental states?

The existing evidence appears to show that children with autism are able to do this—that ID is intact in these children. First, these children use the word "want" in their spontaneous speech (Tager-Flusberg 1989, 1993) and when describing picture stories involving agents (Baron-Cohen, Leslie, and Frith 1986). They say things like "She wants the ice cream" and "He is going to go swimming," identifying desires and goals, respectively. Second, they can distinguish animacy (Baron-Cohen 1991a), which is close to the class of agency, which itself is one of the basic categories that ID picks out. Third, they can understand that desires can cause emotions—that someone who gets what he wants will feel happy, and someone else who does not get what he wants will feel sad (Baron-Cohen 1991b; Phillips 1993; Tan and Harris 1991).[4] For all these reasons, I suggest that ID is probably functioning normally in children with autism. This does not mean that they are able to understand all aspects of desire, or the more complex mental state of intention. (Phillips

(1993) suggests that the latter may be linked to epistemic mental states, such as belief.)

Autism and EDD

In chapter 4 I distinguished the functions EDD has when it is working alone (as in early infancy) from the functions it has when it is connected to SAM (from toddlerhood on). Regarding its early, basic functions, I interpret the existing evidence as showing that EDD may be intact in children with autism.

They are able to detect when a person in a photograph is "looking at them" (Baron-Cohen, Campbell, Karmiloff-Smith, Grant, and Walker, in press). Furthermore, they interpret eye direction in terms of someone's "seeing" something. They use the word "see" in their spontaneous speech (Tager-Flusberg 1993; Baron-Cohen, Leslie, and Frith 1986), and they can work out what someone else is looking at when asked to do so (Hobson 1984; Baron-Cohen 1989a, 1991c; Tan and Harris 1991). This is something of a geometric exercise, and their geometric understanding of gaze direction is quite reasonable. For example, when asked which of three colored pegs a person in a photo is looking at, children with autism can answer correctly both in the easy case shown in the upper panel of figure 5.1 and in the more difficult case shown in the lower panel (Leekam, Baron-Cohen, Perrett, Milders, and Brown 1993).

Thus, the basic functioning of EDD seems to be normal in children with autism. Whether such children show the normal pattern of physiological arousal during eye contact (i.e., when EDD is working) has not yet been studied, however. And, of course, in order to assess the evidence for the more complex functions of EDD in autism, we need to bring in SAM.

Autism and SAM

Recall that SAM's principal function is to build triadic representations, which are needed to specify and verify that the self and another agent are attending to the same object or event. All the

Figure 5.1
Two examples of photos used in the geometric test of eye-direction detection.
Reproduced from Leekam et al. 1993.

available evidence points to a massive impairment in the functioning of SAM in most children with autism.

Children with autism often do not show any of the main
forms of joint-attention behavior. Thus, they do not show gaze
monitoring (Leekam et al. 1993; Mundy et al. 1986; Loveland
and Landry 1986),[5] nor do they show the related behaviors of
attempting to direct the visual attention of others by using the
pointing gesture in its "protodeclarative" form (Baron-Cohen
1989a; Mundy et al. 1986; Curcio 1978). This is not because they
cannot point at all—they do use the pointing gesture for some
other, non-joint attentional functions, such as to request objects
that are out of reach (Baron-Cohen 1989a) and to identify different items in an array, for themselves (Goodhart and Baron-
Cohen 1993). And not only is the protodeclarative pointing gesture missing in young children with autism, but so are other
declarative gestures, such as the showing gesture (which young
normal toddlers use simply to show someone else something of
interest).

I assume that this is not just a deficit of joint visual attention
but, rather, a central problem in the workings of SAM. SAM's
key function is to provide a drive toward establishing what is of
shared interest between the self and another person—to try to
get on to someone else's wavelength, as it were. SAM aims to
build triadic representations in whatever modality it can. In the
blind, who obviously lack EDD, SAM still appears to function,
via touch and hearing, as best it can. Blind children establish
joint attention via touch, by taking one over to an object and
putting one's hand on it. They also direct one to look at something by using the words "see" and "look." Landau and
Gleitman (1985) report that a girl blind from birth produced the
following phrases at the ages noted:

  See? It's in my lap. (36 months)

  Look what I have! (36 months)

  Look how I do it! (36 months)

  See camera! (37 months)

  Look, I got Legos. (39 months)

This blind child also responded correctly to the instructions "Let Mommy see the car" (figure 5.2) and "Make it so Mommy cannot see the car" (figure 5.3), which suggests that, although she could never have had a normal sense of what it means for another person to see an object visually, she had a pretty good idea of what "see" means in an amodal sense: to apprehend, or to explore perceptually, or to have available to one of the sensory modalities (ibid., pp. 75, 77). Indeed, one blind adult gave a wonderful definition of the word "gaze": "To look at something intensely. An equivalent would be to listen to something very hard." (ibid., p. 96)

Figure 5.2
A blind child responding to the instruction "Let mommy see the car." Reproduced from Landau and Gleitman 1985.

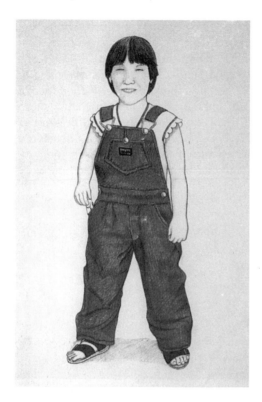

Figure 5.3
A blind child responding to the instruction "Make it so that mommy cannot see the car." Reproduced from Landau and Gleitman 1985.

In most children with autism, SAM does not appear to be working through any modality—vision, touch, or audition. By and large, they bring an object over to someone, or point an object out, or lead someone to an object and place the person's hand on it, only when they want the person to operate that object or to get it for them. This is not shared attention in any sense; these behaviors are primarily instrumental, and do not indicate a desire to share interest with another person for its own sake.

Furthermore, one symptom in autism looks very much like a reflection of a failure to establish joint auditory attention: children with autism often speak too loudly, or too softly, or with little intonational inflection (Frith 1989). I suspect that normal children modulate their intonation to make their speech interesting and audible to the listener, and that children with autism do not because they lack a concept of the other person as an interested listener.

For these reasons, I suggest that in autism the deficit in joint visual attention stems from a deeper impairment in SAM,[6] and that this has two consequences: triadic representations cannot be built in any modality, and there is no output from SAM to trigger ToMM. The prediction that arises from this claim is that in autism virtually all aspects of ToMM should be impaired.

Autism and ToMM

Representing the Full Range of Mental States
If ToMM is dysfunctional in children with autism, then they should clearly have difficulty understanding the epistemic mental state of belief. Dennett (1978b) argued that the best way to test a child's understanding of belief is to investigate if the child can understand that someone might hold a false belief—indeed, he suggested, this might constitute a litmus test of whether an organism had a "theory of mind," in that in such cases it becomes possible to distinguish unambiguously between the child's (true) belief and the child's awareness of someone else's

different (false) belief. Wimmer and Perner (1983) followed this suggestion by designing a "false-belief test," which they used with normal children (figure 5.4). They showed that around the age of 3–4 years normal children pass such a test. Alan Leslie, Uta Frith, and I adapted this test for use with children with autism, children with Down's Syndrome, and normal children (Baron-Cohen, Leslie, and Frith 1985).

The test involves seeing that Sally puts a marble in one place, and that later, while Sally is away, Anne puts the marble some-where else. The child needs to appreciate that, since Sally was absent when her marble was moved from its original location, she won't know it was moved, and therefore must still believe it is in its original location. (Notice the resemblance between this little story and the Snow White fairy tale, in which Snow White

Figure 5.4
A schematic summary of the "Sally–Anne Test" of understanding false belief. (C = child; E = experimenter.) Reproduced from Baron-Cohen, Leslie, and Frith 1985.

was absent when her wicked stepmother put on her disguise and therefore doesn't know that the old woman selling apples at her door is really her wicked stepmother.)

On the test question "Where will Sally look for her marble?" the vast majority of normal children and children with Down's Syndrome passed the test, indicating the original location. But only a small minority of the children with autism did so. Instead, most of them indicated where the marble really was. This pattern of results is also found when the wording of the test question is "Where does Sally think the marble is?" Since the children with autism were older and had a higher "mental age"[7] than the children in either of the two control groups, this study supports the notion that in autism the mental state of belief is poorly understood. This result has now been replicated many times.[8]

Using a totally different test (the "Smarties test"), Perner, Frith, Leslie, and Leekam (1989) got the same basic result. In this test, the child is first shown a familiar Smarties[9] container and is asked "What do you think is in here?" The child naturally replies "Smarties." The child is then shown that the tube actually contains pencils. Next the experimenter closes the tube and asks the child two "belief questions." The first question is "When I first showed you this tube (before we opened it up) what did you think was in here?" The normal child, of course, correctly replies by referring to his or her earlier, now false, belief: "Smarties." The experimenter follows this up with: "And when the next child comes in (who hasn't seen inside the tube), what will he think is inside here?" Again, the normal child correctly replies by referring to the other child's false belief: "Smarties." When Perner et al. gave this task to children with autism, they found that the majority of their subjects answered "Pencils" to the two belief questions. That is, they answered by considering their own knowledge of what was in the box rather than by referring to their own previous false belief or to someone else's current false belief. The robustness of this finding suggests that in autism there is a genuine inability to understand other people's different beliefs.

In another study, Frith, Leslie, and I tested this again, this time using a largely non-verbal method (Baron-Cohen, Leslie, and Frith 1986). We used a picture-sequencing test in which picture stories (each four frames long) depicted, when correctly sequenced, either a character's false belief (figure 5.5), a character's desires and goals (figure 5.6), or a character's causal actions on an inanimate object (figure 5.7). Again, the children with autism performed very poorly on the stories involving an understanding of belief, although they were at least as good as the children with Down's Syndrome or the normal controls at sequencing the stories involving the character's desires and goals. This again shows ID working normally in these children, while ToMM is specifically impaired. The children with autism were also fine at sequencing the stories involving physical causality (which did not require any understanding of mental states). This demonstrated that the autism-specific deficit in understanding beliefs as psychological causes of behavior was not due to general demands of language or to an inability to understand causality. It also ruled out a general sequencing deficit, contrary to earlier reports.[10]

Although most children with autism fail tests of belief understanding, a minority of them pass. This subgroup ranges from 20 to 35 percent in different samples. Moreover, that these subjects tend to be the same subjects in different tests leads to the conclusion that, on the face of it, the members of this "talented minority" (as Uta Frith calls them) have an intact understanding of belief. In a later study, however, this was shown to be the result of a "ceiling effect": passing the Sally–Anne test does not imply that they have a normal ToMM, since most false-belief tests are set at an equivalent mental age of about 3–4 years and the mental ages of the children with autism we tested were well above this (Baron-Cohen 1989b). The task we used in this later study, designed for normal children by Perner and Wimmer (1985), is a more taxing test of belief understanding. To pass it one must understand nested beliefs, or beliefs about beliefs (e.g., "Anne thinks that Sally thinks x")—these being well within the comprehension of normal 6–7-year-olds. Most teenagers with

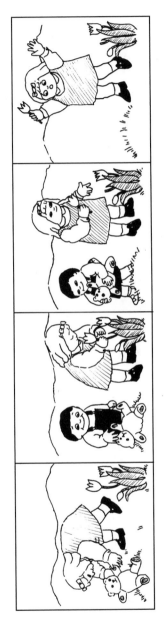

Figure 5.5
Picture-sequencing test involving stories centering on a character's false belief. Adapted from Baron-Cohen, Leslie, and Frith 1986.

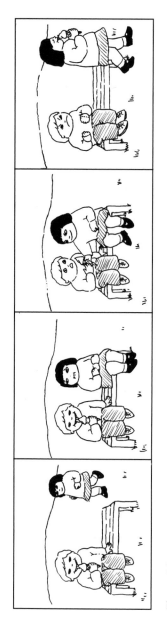

Figure 5.6
Picture-sequencing test involving stories centering on a character's desires and goals. Adapted from Baron-Cohen, Leslie, and Frith 1986.

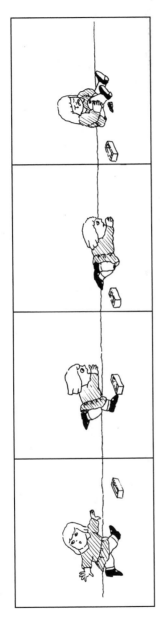

Figure 5.7
Picture-sequencing test involving stories centering on physical causal events. Adapted from Baron-Cohen, Leslie, and Frith 1986.

autism failed this outright, despite having a language level at least equivalent to a 7-year-old's (Ozonoff, Pennington, and Rogers 1991; Holroyd and Baron-Cohen 1993).

Thus, it appears that most children with autism do not understand beliefs at the equivalent level of normal 3–4-year-olds, but some do; yet even the latter show impaired understanding of beliefs at the equivalent level of normal 6–7-year-olds. (A very small minority of individuals with autism pass tests of ToMM even at the 7-year level. I will discuss one such individual in chapter 8, since this raises the question of whether this severe deficit can be overcome or circumvented.)

Understanding knowing appears to be easier than understanding belief for normal children. Why this should be so is not completely clear; however, some authors give as the reason that, since knowledge is true belief, this should be simpler than false belief (as misrepresentation is not involved).

Leslie and Frith (1988) tested whether children with autism understood knowing. The child was shown an actor watching the experimenter hiding a "counter" (a plastic token). When the actor left, the experimenter asked the child to put a second counter in a second hiding place. The child was then asked where the actor would look for a counter on her return. Leslie and Frith found that only about half of the children with autism passed this test by indicating the place the actor knew about rather than the place she was ignorant about. Since only about a quarter of them passed a false-belief task, these findings suggest that understanding knowledge is slightly easier than belief for children with autism, but that the majority of them show deficits in comprehension of both mental states.[11]

If children with autism really have some impairment in the development or functioning of ToMM, they should also have difficulty understanding the mental state of pretending. Most studies that have looked at pretense in autism have not directly tested the subject's comprehension of this mental state; instead they have addressed the question indirectly by means of the following logic: In order to pretend, one must understand how pretending is different from not pretending; therefore, observe whether the child can produce "pretend scenarios" while play-ing. A range of studies now show that in children with autism spontaneous pretend play is severely impoverished or altogeth-er absent.[12]

Building a Theory of Mind
What else might we expect to see, if ToMM was damaged in children with autism? According to the model outlined in chap-ter 4, we should also expect to see that the mentalistic "theory" that normal children possess would be missing or disturbed. For example, we should expect their understanding of some of the basic axioms of the theory to be shaky or absent. One central axiom is that seeing leads to knowing. Given the evidence that understanding knowing seems beyond most children with autism, one might expect this principle to be beyond them. Perner et al. (1989) tested this by showing subjects an object being hidden, but not showing a confederate. They then asked the child who knew what was hidden and who had been allowed to look. Although the vast majority of children with autism passed the "look" question, only about half of them passed the "know" question. Frances Goodhart and I replicated this (Baron-Cohen and Goodhart 1994), using the wonderfully simple method that Pratt and Bryant (1990) had used with nor-mal 3-year-olds. After a subject has seen one of two actors look into the box and the other one simply touch the box (figure 5.8), the subject is asked which of the two actors (or story characters) knows what is in the box. This paradigm thus controls for the child's simply choosing the character who did something to the box. Only a third of children with autism passed this test, where-as three quarters of children with a mental handicap passed.

Additional indirect evidence that this principle poses difficul-ties for children with autism comes from a naturalistic study of deception in autism (Baron-Cohen 1992) in which the child was asked to hide a penny in one hand. Across a series of trials, the children with autism succeeded in keeping the object out of sight but failed to hide the visible clues that would enable the guesser to infer (know) the whereabouts of the penny (e.g., they

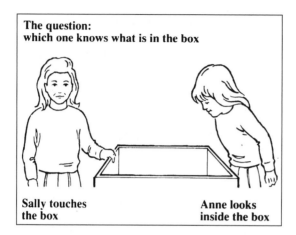

The question:
which one knows what is in the box

Sally touches
the box

Anne looks
inside the box

Figure 5.8
A schematic illustration of the "seeing leads to knowing" test. After Pratt and Bryant 1990.

omitted to close the empty hand, or hid the penny in full view of the guesser, or showed the guesser where the penny was before he had guessed). Children with mental handicap (but not autism) and normal 3-year-olds made far fewer errors of this sort. For them, the game was fun if they succeeded in keeping information about the whereabouts of the penny out of the guesser's mind. This study adds to the data on deception deficits in autism (Oswald and Ollendick 1989; Sodian and Frith 1992, 1993).

A second aspect of the normal child's theory of mind is the ability to apply an understanding of beliefs to the realm of emotion. Normal children can recognize not only simple emotions (such as happiness and sadness) but also belief-based emotions, such as surprise. When we tested this in children with autism, it turned out that they too could recognize the simple emotions, but they had difficulty in recognizing the belief-based emotion of surprise (Baron-Cohen, Spitz, and Cross 1993).[13] Viewing photos like those shown in figure 5.9, most children with autism were able to match happy and sad, but significantly more children with autism made errors in matching pictures of surprised expressions. They sometimes mistook these for non-cognitive states such as yawning or being hungry, focusing on the open mouth.

Some studies have examined the prediction of emotion rather than its recognition. The aim in these studies is to establish how much a child with autism understands about the causes of emotion—how he or she will feel, given a set of causal circumstances. Harris et al. (1989) found that normal 3–4-year-olds understood that emotion can be caused by situations (e.g., nice situations make you feel happy, nasty ones make you feel sad) and desires (e.g., fulfilled desires make you feel happy, unfulfilled ones make you feel sad). They also found that by the age of 4–6 years normal children understood that beliefs can affect emotion (e.g., if you think you're getting what you want, you'll feel happy, and if you think you're not, you'll feel sad—irrespective of what you're actually getting).

When I tested whether children with autism were able to judge a story character's emotion when this was caused by a situation, a desire, or a belief (Baron-Cohen 1991b), I found that they could understand situations as causes of emotion, and that they were as good as a group of mentally handicapped children at predicting the character's emotion on the basis of the character's desire. However, they were significantly worse than either normal 5-year-olds or mentally handicapped children at predicting the character's emotion on the basis of the character's belief.

A third aspect of the normal child's theory of mind is the understanding that the brain is an organ with mental functions. In one experiment (Baron-Cohen 1989d), after it was established that they knew the location of the brain, children with autism were asked what they thought the brain was for. In reply, most of them referred to its role in behavior ("It makes you move," etc.). Only a small proportion of them referred to its mentalistic role ("It's for thinking," etc.), even after considerable prompting. In contrast, most of a group of mentally handicapped children and most normal 5-year-olds referred to the brain's mental function (dreaming, remembering, keeping things secret, etc.).

Figure 5.9
Examples of photographs used in the test of matching expressions of emotion.
Reproduced from Fairburn System of Visual References (1978).

Another cornerstone of the normal child's theory of mind is the ontological distinction between mental and physical entities. Wellman and Estes (1986) found that normal 3-year-olds had a stable grasp of this distinction. I adopted their method for use with children with autism (Baron-Cohen 1989d). The subject was told a story about two characters: one who had an object and one who was thinking (or dreaming, or pretending, or remembering) about an object. After each story, the subject was asked to make judgements about which character could perform an action on the object—e.g., "Which one can touch the [object]?" Most of the normal children (and most of those with a mental handicap) passed the test, by indicating that it is the one who has the object who can touch it, etc. Only a small proportion of the children with autism did so.[14]

If ToMM is damaged in autism, then children with autism should also have difficulty in distinguishing appearance and reality. Flavell, Green, and Flavell (1986) showed that, when presented with misleading objects such as a sponge painted to look like a rock, normal children between 4 and 6 years of age could say not only what it looks like (a rock) but also what it really is (a sponge). In doing so, they distinguished between their initial (perception-based) belief about the object and their current knowledge about it. How would children with autism perform on such a test?

Using the method of Flavell et al., I found that, while most mental handicapped children and most normal subjects were able to answer an appearance question ("What does it look like?") and a reality question ("What is it really?") correctly, once again only a small percentage of subjects with autism were able to do so (Baron-Cohen 1989d). When shown objects with misleading appearances, such as a stone that looked like an egg, most children without autism were able to say (e.g.) "It looks like an egg, but really it's a stone." In contrast, most children with autism made largely "phenomenist" errors, saying "It looks like an egg," "It really is an egg," and similar things. They seemed to be dominated by their perception, and unable to consider their knowledge.[15]

In discussing the appearance-reality distinction, Flavell et al. (1986, pp. 1–20) wrote:

> It is probably a universal outcome in our species. This knowledge seems so necessary to everyday intellectual and social life that one can hardly imagine a society in which normal people would not acquire it. . . . Knowledge about the distinction seems to presuppose the explicit knowledge that human beings are sentient, cognizing subjects . . . It is part of the larger development of our conscious knowledge about our own and other minds.

If, as appears to be the case, most children with autism really are unaware of the appearance-reality distinction, as well as being blind to their own past thoughts and to other people's possibly different thoughts, their world must be largely dominated by current perceptions and sensations. Further, much of the social world must appear unpredictable and therefore even frightening. In terms of the model, the deficits in SAM and

ToMM appear to have widespread but highly specific and pre-dictable conceptual ramifications for children with autism. The consequences discussed here are undoubtedly only a small sub-set of these; the complete consequences for their cognitive devel-opment remain to be explored.

ToMM in Children and Adults with Congenital Blindness

From my earlier claims about blind children, one would predict that if SAM is intact in such children then ToMM should also be intact. One might expect blindness to delay the functioning of SAM, since the only input that is available to a blind child comes via ID, and thus it comes as no surprise that a proportion of con-genitally blind children initially show some "autistic" features (Hobson 1990; Fraiberg 1977). However, such delays and obsta-cles to the functioning of SAM clearly should not prevent its eventual functioning, since SAM is held to be intact in such indi-viduals. That ToMM is indeed intact in blind people is obvious from the apparent ability of blind adults to participate normally in social relationships. Some specific evidence comes, again, from an interview with a blind adult, who was asked to define some mentalistic concepts and who defined "to notice" as fol-lows:

> To see something that comes into your view. But not only to see it but to perceive it and understand it. You could sit on this rocking chair and not notice the color of it at all. Might have to be looking at something specifically to notice it. (Landau and Gleitman 1985, p. 96)

SAM should be intact even in an adult who was born both deaf and blind, although its use would obviously rely heavily on tac-tile information. In such cases, SAM should therefore be able to trigger ToMM. Here is a definition of "to stare" supplied by one such adult:

> Well, stare means to stare at a person or an object, maybe in surprise or maybe spellbound. For instance, when some-body says something to you and you are shocked at what

> you heard, you stare at the person as if you are asking a
> person a question, because you can't believe what he has
> just said. Or to stare, because you are concentrating more
> deeply into an object. So, you will stare at it, trying to focus
> your mind on what you are looking at. (reported by C.
> Chomsky [1984]; cited in Landau and Gleitman 1985)

As the theory predicts, the language of individuals born blind is
beautifully laced with the full range of mental-state terms.
Tragically, they are missing in the language (Tager-Flusberg
1993) and in the thought of most individuals with autism.

Chapter 6
How Brains Read Minds

A fundamental tenet of evolutionary biology is that there are no sudden qualitative jumps from one species to the next. The human brain is remarkably similar to those of lower primates. Mentalizing abilities did not suddenly develop from nothing. Such abilities result from relatively small improvements in existing mechanisms. In order to understand mentalizing abilities and their relation to the brain we need to identify the precursors of these abilities in animals. (C. Frith, in press)

The mindreading system has, according to the theory I proposed in chapter 4, four separate mechanisms or subcomponents. ID and EDD receive perceptual input directly; SAM and ToMM are more central. So far, I have discussed these four mechanisms only at the cognitive level. The cognitive level is essentially the functional level, and these descriptions typically refer to the flow and processing of information, and how that information is represented. The cognitive level of description is also an example of how scientists adopt what Dennett calls the "Design Stance" (see chapter 3 above) when attempting to work out how the mind functions.

In principle, the cognitive description of the mindreading system that I have given could be a description of an organism with "natural intelligence" (e.g., *Homo sapiens*), or it could be a description of an "artificially" intelligent system (a robot or a computer). This is because cognitive mechanisms, described in their own right, are only about things like information flow, information processing, and representations of information.

It is now time to talk about the instantiation of these cognitive mechanisms in something real—time to adopt what Dennett calls the Physical Stance. Since we are considering real people here, we of course need to think about how the cognitive description of the mindreading system (outlined above) is instantiated in the human neural system. Therefore, we must explore the "wetware"—the brain itself. Just how does the brain allow us to read minds?

The Introspection Organ

So far, the only proposal on the table has come from Humphrey (1986, 1993), who suggests that our capacity for mindreading is due entirely to the evolution of an "inner eye" for introspecting on our own mental states. Here is his argument:

> Imagine first the case of an animal that does not have an inner eye. It has sense organs that monitor the outside world, limbs which allow it to operate in and on its environment, and at the center a sophisticated information-processor and decision-maker. But it has no insight into anything which is happening inside its brain. It is, in short, an unconscious Cartesian machine [see figure 6.1].
>
> Now imagine that at some time in history a new kind of sense organ evolves, the inner eye whose field of view is

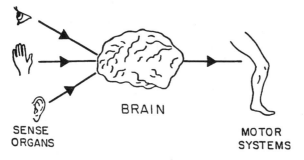

Figure 6.1
Humphrey's diagram of an entity lacking insight. Reproduced from Humphrey 1993.

not the outside world but the brain itself. Like other sense organs, the inner eye provides a picture of its information field that is partial and selective; but equally like other sense organs it has been designed by evolution so that its picture is a useful one, a "user-friendly" description which tells the subject just so much as he requires to know in a form that he is predisposed to understand—allowing him by a kind of magical translation to see his own brain states as conscious states of mind [see figure 6.2].

If we compare these two at a purely behavioral level, the unconscious and the conscious animal might be in most ways indistinguishable. Both could be highly intelligent; both might show emotional behavior, moods, passions, and so on. But while for the unconscious animal the behavior would just happen as if its brain were effectively on auto-pilot, for the conscious one every intelligent action would be accompanied by the awareness of the thought processes involved, every perception by an accompanying sensation, every emotion by a feeling. (Humphrey 1986, pp. 39–40)

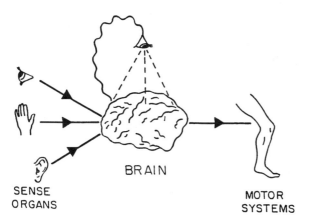

BRAIN

SENSE
ORGANS

MOTOR
SYSTEMS

Figure 6.2
Humphrey's diagram of an entity possessing insight. Reproduced from Humphrey 1993.

Humphrey's proposal makes a lot of intuitive sense. We are aware of our thoughts and feelings, and "inner eye" is as good a term for this awareness as any. And our reluctance to credit other animals with such an awareness gives Humphrey's evolutionary story plausibility. It stops well short of a neuroscientific account, however.

The neural theory I will be outlining in this chapter is that the mindreading system is instantiated in a three-node brain circuit involving the superior temporal sulcus, the orbito-frontal cortex, and the amygdala. This theory builds on earlier work (Baron-Cohen and Ring 1994; Brothers 1990). At this stage it must be taken as speculative and therefore tentative, in view of the many gaps in the evidence. Nevertheless, as an exercise in evolutionary psychology and cognitive neuroscience, I feel obliged to at least address the question of where in the brain the mindreading system might be located. I will unfold this neural circuit by discussing the place in it of each of the cognitive components of the mindreading system. I will begin by considering the brain basis of EDD and ToMM, since there is more evidence about their brain basis than there is for the other two mechanisms.

EDD and the Brain

From the current evidence, EDD appears to be localized in the superior temporal sulcus (STS) and in the amygdala. Figures 6.3

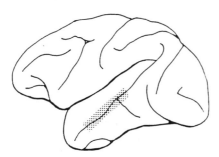

Figure 6.3
The superior temporal sulcus. Adapted from Brothers 1990.

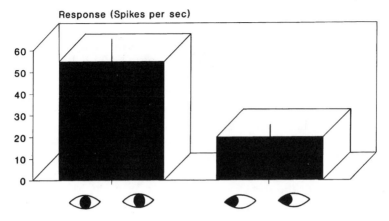

Response (Spikes per sec)

Figure 6.4
Data suggesting that M047, a cell assembly in the superior temporal sulcus of the monkey brain, "fires" significantly more when the animal is looking at the eyes of another animal (single-cell recording). Adapted from Perrett and Mistlin 1990.

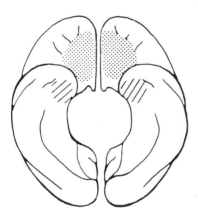

Figure 6.5
Dotted area: the orbito-frontal cortex. Hatched area: the amygdala. Adapted from Brothers 1990.

and 6.5 show these areas of the brain. The evidence for these claims is as follows.

First, in the early 1980s a number of researchers identified areas of temporal cortex which appeared to contain "face" cells (Bruce, Desimone, and Gross 1981; Perrett, Rolls, and Cann 1982) on the basis of findings that when their electrical activity was measured while the animal (usually a monkey) was observing a face these cells "fired" significantly more than cells in neighboring areas of cortex, and more than they themselves did to other kinds of stimuli. Later, Perrett and co-workers (1985, 1990) identified specific cells in the STS that appeared to respond selectively to the direction of gaze. For example, M047, a cell assembly in the STS, was found to fire more when the animal was looking at the eyes of another animal (figure 6.4). Other cells in the STS have been shown to demonstrate the opposite pattern. Perrett and his colleagues refer to the cells that respond to gaze direction as "cells responsive to the state of attention of the other individual" and suggest that these cells have the primary function of detecting whether another individual is "looking at me." In the model I presented in chapter 4, these cells would correspond to the primitive functions of EDD (prior to its being connected to SAM).

A second line of evidence for EDD's being located in the STS comes from studies of animals and human patients with acquired brain damage. For example, lesions in the STS in the monkey brain produce an impairment in the ability to discriminate gaze direction (Campbell et al. 1990), and the same is true of some human patients with prosopagnosia (a disorder that affects different aspects of face processing in different patients) (Perrett et al. 1991; Campbell et al. 1990; Heywood and Cowey 1991).

The claim that EDD lies on a circuit between the STS and the amygdala derives from additional evidence that the medial and lateral nuclei of the amygdala have face-sensitive cells (Leonard et al. 1985; Nakamura, Mikami, and Kubota 1992) and cells sensitive to eye direction (Brothers, Ring, and Kling 1990). Of course, cells in the amygdala have other functions, such as responding to facial expressions of emotion, but here we are just considering the evidence relevant to EDD. Naturally, for it to make any sense that EDD lies in two different nodes within a circuit spanning the STS and the amygdala, there must be key neural connections between the these two regions of the brain. Neuroanatomical studies demonstrate the presence of such connections from the STS to the lateral nucleus of the amygdala (Aggleton, Burton, and Passingham 1980). Recent accounts of animals with lesions (damage) in the amygdala suggest that this produces difficulties in social perception (Kling and Brothers 1992).

The evidence discussed so far clearly suggests a neural basis for EDD. The evidence for the localization of SAM is not so clear. The model assumes that EDD must be linked to SAM, and SAM must be linked to ToMM. There is some evidence that ToMM may be located in a third node in the circuit: the orbito-frontal cortex (OFC). Certainly there are direct inputs from the STS to the OFC (Barbas 1988) and from the medial structures of the amygdala to the OFC (Aggleton 1985; Van Hoesen 1981; Porrino, Crane, and Goldman-Rakic 1982; Amaral and Price 1984).

ToMM and the Brain

Regarding the location of ToMM, I want first to describe the evidence pointing to the OFC. As figure 6.5 shows, the OFC lies on the ventral surface of the frontal lobes, in a position corresponding to what the neurologist Brodmann (1925) identified as areas 10–14 in his "map" of the human brain.

The first line of evidence comes from human patients with acquired damage to the OFC. One such patient, referred to by his initials, EVR, was described by the neurologists Paul Eslinger and Antonio Damasio (1985). At the age of 35 years, EVR was discovered to have a cancerous growth (a meningioma) in the OFC of his brain. In the ensuing operation, the surgeon removed all of the right side of his OFC and part of the left side. There was, naturally, some damage to adjacent areas.

Before the operation, EVR appeared to have been socially normal, doing well at work and with a family of his own. After the operation, he began behaving in such a way that his family and those who knew him well described his as having lost his social judgement. Eslinger and Damasio (ibid.) use the term "acquired sociopathy." Other patients with similar lesions appear to fit the same picture (Ackerley and Benton 1948; Damasio, Tranel, and Damasio 1990). Since "social sense" or social judgement would appear to require ToMM, this neurological evidence is at least consistent with the idea that ToMM is located in the OFC. Other patients with OFC lesions who have undergone explicit tests of ToMM have performed rather poorly (Price et al. 1990). Similarly, patients with damage to the OFC have performed poorly on tests of the pragmatics of language (Kaczmarek 1984; Alexander, Benson, and Stuss 1987), which would appear to require ToMM (Baron-Cohen 1988; Happé 1994; Roth and Leslie 1991; Tager-Flusberg 1993). Such patients are also reported to be "unaware of their predicament" (Damasio and Tranel 1988), which would also suggest a failure in the ability to self-reflect.

The second line of evidence for ToMM's being located in the OFC comes from a neuroimaging study (Baron-Cohen, Ring, Moriarty, Schmitz, Costa, and Ell 1994) in which each of a number of normal adult volunteers were asked to lie down on a bed, with his or her head in a SPECT[1] brain scanner. The subject was asked to listen to words played through headphones, and in particular to listen for words describing the mind or what the mind can do (think, know, pretend, imagine, hope, fear, remember, plan, intend, want, dream, etc.). These mental-state terms were randomly mixed with other words in the list, so the subject had to listen carefully to find them. (This turned out to be an easy task, since these were all normal adults who were therefore used to mindreading.) In a comparison task, we asked the same subjects to listen to a new list of words, but this time to pick out words describing the body or what the body can do. These were words like teeth, blood, walk, face, toes, and eat. (This time, the list contained no mental-state terms.) We found that when the subjects were picking out the mental-state terms, there was increased activation (as reflected by increased blood flow) in the OFC, relative to other frontal areas, and this was particularly true of the right OFC, relative to the left frontal polar (LFP) region. Although this test taps only one aspect of ToMM, it is again consistent with the earlier evidence suggesting that ToMM is located in the OFC.

Finally, animal studies show that lesions in the OFC lead to loss of social status and changes in social behavior (Butter and Snyder 1972). In contrast, other frontal-lobe lesions do not produce such significant social changes in experimental animals (de Bruin 1990).

ID, SAM, and the Brain

In discussing the OFC-STS-amygdala circuit as the seat of the mindreading system, I have not specified a particular basis for SAM, which I envisaged in chapter 4 as one of the four key components of the mindreading system. This is because at present there are very few clues as to where this particular component might be situated, in contrast with the previous two mechanisms. One might expect that SAM is supported by the STS, given its close functional link with EDD, but this is a question for future research.[2]

There is some evidence suggesting that ID may be localized in the STS. This comes, again, from the single-cell recording studies conducted by Perrett et al. (1991), who found that specific cells in the STS fire significantly more often when the animal observes an agent doing something. This can be thought of as part of ID in that almost any detection of action will involve attributing a goal or a desire to an agent. Perrett and co-workers have also found cells in the same region of the cortex that respond to self-propelled motion (such as an animal reaching toward something). Again, among the stimulus features that trigger ID, self-propelled motion is a key property that is read in terms of goals and desires.

Finally, as was mentioned in chapter 4, there is some evidence from adult patients with brain damage that the ability to distinguish agents and non-agents, a key function of ID, is impaired (Warrington and Shallice 1984).[3]

Autism and the Brain

Let us now consider the possibility that a lesion—that is, damage of some sort—in the OFC-STS-amygdala circuit could produce autism, since this should follow from the twin claims that this circuit is dedicated to mindreading and that children with autism are mindblind.

At present, not much is known about the site or sites of brain damage in autism. That there is brain damage in autism is no longer disputed (Bailey 1993), but the site of this damage is unclear because of what can only be described as contradictory evidence. Thus, some studies find damage in one place in some patients with autism, while other studies find damage in completely different places in the brain in other patients with autism.

In what follows, I shall pick my way through this evidence, in order to highlight those studies that are consistent with the idea that autism is produced by a break at some point in the proposed OFC-STS-amygdala circuit.[4] Some studies show evidence of frontal-lobe dysfunction (Piven et al. 1990; Horwitz et al. 1988), others show evidence of temporal-lobe dysfunction (DeLong 1978; Hauser, DeLong, and Rosman 1975); yet others show evidence of amygdala dysfunction (Bauman and Kemper 1985, 1988). Of course, though these studies appear to fit my model nicely, the evidence is not so tidy. For example, these studies do not specify in which regions within the frontal or temporal lobes the lesion or abnormality may lie, whereas my model specifies the OFC and the STS with a degree of precision. In addition, there are other studies in which the abnormalities do not lie on the circuit I have suggested.[5] Establishing whether these latter abnormalities are central to the mindreading system will be a difficult but important task.

Nevertheless, I suspect that two reasons why previous attempts at localization of brain damage in autism lacked some precision are that those studies were not hypothesis-driven and did not employ as fine-grained a method as was used in the single-cell recording studies mentioned earlier in this chapter. Finally, different subgroups of autism might result from different lesions in different parts of the proposed circuit (Baron-Cohen and Ring 1994).

Certainly, from studies of the effects of lesions in these three areas, we might expect a different set of symptoms to ensue from each type of damage. For example, if the damage were in the OFC, we would expect typical OFC symptoms: impaired social judgement, "utilization" behavior (where a patient cannot keep from using an object, even when the context for doing so is not relevant), abnormal pragmatics of language, diminished aggression, indifference, a diminished appreciation of danger, hyper-olfactory exploration, and excessive activity. All these symptoms have been documented as effects of OFC lesions (Baron-Cohen and Ring 1994), and all are commonly seen in autism.

Similarly, if the damage was in the amygdala, one would expect to see typical amygdala symptoms: abnormalities in social perception, failure to attach emotional significance to stimuli, and diminution of aggression, fear, and affiliative behavior. All these symptoms are evident in patients with amygdala lesions (Kling and Brothers 1992). Again, these all commonly occur in autism. Finally, if the lesion was in the STS, we would expect deficits not only in EDD but also in related face-processing tasks. And, depending on the extent of the damage to the temporal lobe, we might also expect difficulties in language (since the language-comprehension center, called Wernicke's area, is also temporal). These problems too are common in autism.

The Idea of the "Social Brain"

In a very important article, Leslie Brothers (1990) proposed that we should think about the brain as a "social brain." By this she meant that it—or parts of it—had evolved in order to enable the organism to make sense of and react to the social world.

Brothers' idea, very simply, was that it made considerable sense to expect to find specialized circuits in the brain dedicated to identifying and responding to other animals' emotional states, identities (face, voice), and behavior toward the self or toward other animals (dedicated to ensuring that the animal could participate in and take advantage of the benefits of a social existence). In a later paper (Brothers and Ring 1992) she extended this idea to suggest that there might be a "social module." How does this idea relate to the model of the mindreading system that I have been advancing in this book?

One possibility is that I am wrong, and that there is no specialized mindreading system, and only a more general social module. I happen to think this is not correct, as the evidence from autism that I presented in the last chapter leads to the conclusion that certain aspects of social information processing in these individuals are intact and preserved (notably those involving ID, some basic aspects of EDD, and a range of face-processing skills (Baron-Cohen 1994b, 1995c)), while other aspects of social information processing (notably those that involve SAM and ToMM) are severely impaired. Such dissociability suggests that the mindreading system is to some extent independent of other aspects of social understanding.

A second possibility is that the mindreading system is a part of the social module. This, it seems to me, must be correct, in that mindreading is by definition a system for use within the social environment. In this respect there is no incompatibility between my model and that of Brothers. Rather, as different cases of neuropathology are studied in more detail, we are likely to see that different patterns of neurocognitive dysfunction within the social brain are possible. Equally, some unusual cases of superior functioning of the social brain may be found. This may be true of children with Williams Syndrome (a condition of genetic origin in which the metabolism of calcium is impaired, which results in a pattern of poor cognitive skills against a backdrop of excellent language, face-processing, and mindreading skills). A full characterization of the psychology and neurobiology of the social brain will be an important task for the future.[6]

Chapter 7

The Language of the Eyes

> Imagine you walk into a crowded train. You see a remaining empty seat, so you go across and sit down. You get out your book, and settle into it. During the journey, you become aware of a feeling that someone is looking at you. You glance along the carriage and, sure enough, someone is looking at you. As soon as you make eye contact with this stranger, he looks away. To my mind, this phenomenon is rather striking, in that it is not immediately obvious how you would have known that someone was looking at you, if you were already engaged in another activity. (Baron-Cohen 1994a)

When I step back from the model of the mindreading system that I have proposed, EDD seems to stand out.[1] It is not that EDD is the most important of the components in the mindreading system; one could make a good case that it is SAM. (Just look what happens when a child fails to develop an SAM in the normal way: the outcome of autism seems to be a high risk.) But there is something rather special about EDD. In this chapter, I want to try to convey what that something is.

To recap: EDD is the Eye-Direction Detector. This does not sound like a very graceful or romantic name. Indeed, it sounds rather cold, geometric, precise, and lacking in feeling. But when we look more closely at this mechanism, and how it is used, I think the opposite of these adjectives will be seen to apply.

The Evolution of EDD

As was outlined in chapter 4, EDD's most primitive function is to discern whether another organism's eyes are directed at you.

This apparently simple computation seems to carry considerable emotional value. When you notice that another's eyes are looking at you (as in figure 7.1), your heart rate starts to soar, and this physiological arousal can be measured in the brain's electrical activity, deep in the brain stem (Wada 1961; Nichols and Champness 1971).

It makes good evolutionary sense that we should be hypersensitive to when another organism is watching us, since this is about the best "early warning system" that another organism may be about to attack us, or may be interested in us for some other reason. When one thinks about the evolution of EDD across the animal kingdom, it makes even more sense, since many predators can see their prey clearly from considerable distances. The lion can see its prey from almost a mile away.[2] The hawk is also renowned for its keen vision, which is estimated to be equivalent to that of a human being using binoculars with a magnification of 8X. Many other birds also have vision this good. (Think of how birds of prey swoop down on their victims, often from considerable heights.) Other animals, of course, have considerably worse visual acuity. (For example, the elephant and the rhinoceros can see only about 100 feet.) But, despite the vari-

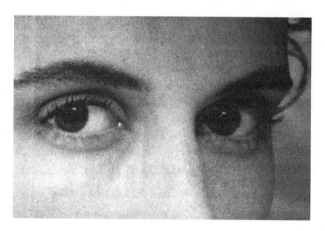

Figure 7.1
Eyes looking directly at you.

ability in predators' visual acuity, from the prey's perspective it is not hard to imagine why evolution might have come up with a mechanism alerting you to react to another's eyes as if they might be good enough to see you.[3]

In Lower Animals

Just how old is EDD, in evolutionary terms? There is some evidence that EDD may go back phylogenetically at least as far as the birds and the reptiles. For example, Ristau (1990, 1991) carried out some elegant experiments testing whether plovers were sensitive to eye direction and whether they reacted to eyes directed at them as a threat. The birds were observed in the dunes on the beaches of Long Island, where they nest. Ristau used two human intruders; one looked toward the dunes and the other looked toward the ocean. Each intruder walked up and down the same path, along the coastline, about 15–25 meters from the dunes. Trials began when an incubating parent plover was on her nest. Ristau found that the birds moved off and stayed off their nests for longer periods when the intruder was gazing toward the dunes than when the intruder was gazing toward the ocean. Moving away from the nest was interpreted as a sign that the parent bird was attempting to lead the intruder away from the nest. Ristau interpreted this as evidence that these birds are capable of detecting if an intruder is looking at them (on their nest) and that they react to gaze so directed as a threat.[4] Furthermore, Scaife (1976) demonstrated that white leghorn chicks show maximum avoidance to two tracking eyelike shapes, and Blest (1957) found that eye spots on the wings of butterflies appeared to elicit an avoidance response in the birds that prey on them.

Snakes too have been reported to be sensitive specifically to eye direction as a cue to a potential threat (Burghardt 1990). For example, if an intruder is about one meter from a hog-nosed snake and looks directly at the snake, the snake will "feign death" for longer than if the intruder averts its eyes. Chickens too go still for a longer time in the presence of a human who is staring at them than in the presence of one who is not looking at them (Gallup, Cummings, and Nash 1972). The phenomenon of tonic immobility has also been documented in lizards, blue crabs, and ducks.[5]

In Mammals and Primates

Most mammals and primates do not react to the eyes with tonic immobility, but nevertheless react with avoidance and fear. For example, macaque monkeys look less at photographic slides of faces with eye contact than at slides of faces with no eye contact (Keating and Keating 1982) and show more emotional distur- bance when confronted by a picture of a full face with eye con- tact than when confronted with a picture of a face turned away to profile with gaze averted (Mendelsohn, Haith, and Goldman- Rakic 1982). Perrett and Mistlin (1990) further demonstrated that appeasement behaviors (lip smacking and teeth chattering) by macaques are controlled by gaze angle and head posture, in that they occur more often in response to a human face looking directly at the animal than in response to a human face tilted backward. (Appeasement behaviors signify fear.)

Mutual gazing, particularly staring, is a well-documented component of threatening displays in many non-human pri- mates. Adult male baboons, macaques, and a number of other Old World monkeys and apes use and react to eye contact as threatening (Hall and Devore 1964; Schaller 1964; Altmann 1967; van Hooff 1962). Chance (1967) describes how, when two ani- mals are threatening each other, the struggle for dominance often ends only when one animal averts its gaze. Chance calls this a "visual cut-off," noting that it may be a mechanism for reducing the physiological arousal produced by direct gaze.

Recognizing that another animal is watching you need not be only a form of threat detection. It also tells you that the other ani- mal is interested in you, and this may be for pro-social reasons. For example, eye contact occurs as part of grooming, greeting, and play in Old World monkeys and apes (van Hooff 1962). We must, of course, be cautious in discussing species-specific differ- ences in the use of a mechanism like EDD, both to avoid lumping different monkey and ape species together and to avoid losing sight of the complexity of the issues at hand. For example, de Waal's observations reveal that, whereas chimpanzees behave in a fully reconciled manner toward former opponents only when eye contact has been made, rhesus monkeys do the opposite: "Both humans and apes avoid eye contact during strained situations and seek it when ready to reconcile. Rhesus monkeys, in contrast, look each other straight in the eye during conflict; dominants intimidate subordinates by fixedly staring at them. Since prolonged eye contact is ominous in their communication, it is logical that they carefully avert their gaze during friendly approaches, including reconciliation." (De Waal 1989, p. 114)

The Functions of EDD and SAM: Are We Both Looking at the Same Thing?

So far, we have been discussing only the primitive detection of (and response to) dyadic eye contact—that is, when two animals are looking directly at one another, in the eyes. But what about the more complex function of detecting whether you and another animal are both looking at the same thing? This was discussed in chapter 4 in relation to the use that SAM makes of EDD. This ability is important because the other animal may have spotted something worth knowing about: a food source, a rival, a mate, or a predator. Here it would pay for you to be able to identify not only what the other animal is looking at but also whether the other animal has recognized that you have seen what it is looking at. It would seem that in the higher primates EDD, thanks to its connection with SAM, has this additional function. For example, both chimpanzees and humans have been observed to use another's eye direction to search for a hidden object in a location being looked at (Menzel and Halperin 1975), and to use their own gaze to direct others' attention away from food sources (Byrne and Whiten 1991). Chimpanzees have also been documented to look in the same direction as other chimps. Such gaze monitoring is also seen in baboons (Cheney and Seyfarth 1990). Whether gaze monitoring in other primates is the same as in humans is not clear.[6]

Although the chief benefit of gaze monitoring is presumably that it reveals whether another animal has spotted something of interest, Gòmez (1991) suggests that another function of EDD among higher primates derives from their understanding not only that eyes can see but also that "attentional contact" is needed for basic communication, such as when one animal is requesting the help of another in a task that the first animal cannot solve alone.

Finally, Chance (1956, 1967) argues that in primates eye direction reveals the social structure: infants attend to their mothers, mothers to their mates, mates to the more dominant males, and so on, all the way up the social hierarchy. This behavior, which Chance calls the "attention structure," may function to maintain a stable social hierarchy without the need for frequent aggressive interactions. That is to say, monitoring who is looking at who gives any member of the group an instant, non-verbal summary of who to defer to, who not to threaten, and who is allied with who. Gaze gives an instant snapshot of social status in a group. Such information may be invaluable as a way of avoiding threatening established hierarchies accidentally, since this carries the risk of retaliation.

To get more of a flavor of the evolution of EDD in primates, consider its use in the following scenario, which involves an encounter between Alex, who has just entered a new social group, and Thalia, with whom Alex is keen to become acquainted:

> Alex stared at Thalia until she turned and almost caught him looking at her. He glanced away immediately, and then she stared at him until his head began to turn toward her. She [quickly looked toward the ground], but as soon as Alex looked away, her gaze returned to him. They went on like this for more than fifteen minutes, always with split-second timing. Finally, Alex managed to catch Thalia looking at him. He made the friendly eyes . . . [and then] approached [her]. (Leakey and Lewin 1992, pp. 287–288)[7]

You could be forgiven for assuming that this couple was human. In fact, Alex and Thalia are members of a troop of baboons that live near Eburru Cliffs, 100 miles northwest of Nairobi, on the floor of the Great Rift Valley. The above observation was made by Barbara Smuts, a primatologist at the University of Michigan, who studied the social life of this troop over several years. Discussing this particular social interaction, Smutts comments that "it was like watching two novices in a singles bar" (Leakey and Lewin 1992, p. 288) In this example we see the "split-second timing" of eye-direction detection, as one animal checks to see if the other is looking at it and each tries to avoid making the other aware that it is checking.

Like baboons, humans appear very accurate at identifying when someone is looking at them. Since there may be only a small difference in geometric angle between your being looked at and something next to you being looked at, the psychophysics of EDD are likely to be impressive. (This remains to be studied in detail in a range of species.) The example of Alex and Thalia also shows how in some species there is a risk that eye contact from a stranger can be misinterpreted as threatening, and how if one's intentions are prosocial (as Alex's were), eye contact must be offered in small doses at the start of such an encounter if this risk is to be avoided.

EDD and SAM in Humans

Mentalistic Interpretation of Gaze
Dyadic eye contact is detected by children and adults with equal ease (Thayer 1977). And, as in other animals, direct eye contact triggers an increase in physiological arousal in humans (Nichols and Champness 1971; Gale et al. 1972; McBride, King, and James 1965). But when we experience increased physiological arousal as a result of eye contact, this is not just experienced. It is also interpreted. We ask ourselves questions like "Why is he looking at me?" Usually, of course, we answer such reflective questions in terms of whether the eye contact signals friendly or hostile intentions. Indeed, we seem to be rather good at distinguishing friendly from hostile eye contact.

So much for the "friend versus foe" interpretation of dyadic eye contact. Regarding SAM's use of EDD to establish shared attention, it is clear that as soon as we notice that someone has rapidly shifted his or her eye direction away from us (as in figure 7.2) we invariably turn to follow what the other person is looking at. At least, humans older than about 9 months do so. This is not some mindless reflex. We can inhibit this response if it is important to do so. Usually, however, we do find ourselves looking in the same direction as another person, and we are aware of consciously noting what the other person is looking at. We ask ourselves questions like "Why is he looking at that?" and "What is he **interested** in?" It is not clear that non-human animals engage in this reflective stance after joint attention, perhaps because in the human case SAM links EDD to ID and ToMM. Thus, in the last interpretation of eye direction, I referred to the other person's state of interest, and this seems like a natural reading of gaze. Interest, of course, is a mental state. I want to suggest that it is the link with ID and ToMM that allows EDD the function of reading gaze in terms of mental states.

To continue this line of argument: In the dyadic example in figure 7.1, it is equally natural for us to read this in terms of "Is he **interested** in me?" This then begs the next question: "Why?" Questions about one mental state are usually answered in terms

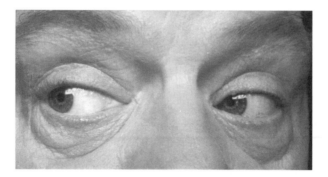

Figure 7.2
Eyes looking away at something else.

of another mental state or a set of such states. Thus, we might read a person's dyadic eye contact in terms of his or her interest, which is itself a function of the other's goals, motives, intentions, and desires. For example, we might think

Maybe he **wants** to attack me,

or

Maybe she **likes** me,

or

Maybe she's **trying** to draw my **attention** to her,

or

Maybe she's **intending to refer** to x.

In our studies of young children (Baron-Cohen, Campbell, Karmiloff-Smith, Grant, and Walker, in press), it is clear that gaze direction is read in terms of these mental states. If a person is looking at something, this is interpreted as an object that he or she may desire, or plan to act upon next, etc. This is not a quirk of early development either: it remains a powerful way that we interpret another's gaze, even as adults (Argyle 1972).

The interpretation of gaze in terms of the mental state of attention is, I think, particularly interesting. Attention is the most immediate mental state that we associate with eye direction. What makes it interesting is the fact that attention can be directed either outward (as in seeing) or inward (as in seeing something in the mind's eye, or imagining something, or thinking about something). This gives us the clue that when a person's eye direction does not appear to be directed at any external object in particular—for example, when a person's eyes are directed upward and away from us but there is no external target in that part of the person's visual field—we rapidly infer that the person is thinking about something unobservable. This mentalistic inference is also drawn effortlessly by young children (Baron-Cohen and Cross 1992). Thus, when we presented pairs of photographs (two examples of which are shown in figures 7.3 and 7.4) to 3-4-year-olds, they had no difficulty at all in identifying "Which one is thinking?" simply on the basis of the person's eye direction. In the 1960s and the 1970s, a great deal of research was conducted on "laterality effects"—whether when someone was thinking about a verbal problem, or a visuospatial problem, his or her gaze moved either right or left, respectively (Gur, Gur, and Harris 1975; Galin and Ornstein 1974). These studies, at the very least, confirm that the activity of thinking is associated with gaze directed away from the other person.

So far, my discussion of how we read the language of the eyes has concentrated very much on the correspondence between the intentionality of mental states and the fact that gaze has direction—that it is about something. In one sense, this sounds circular. As Franz von Brentano (1874) noted, things that have intentionality are things that are directed toward something else; thus, gaze should, of course, have some properties of intentionality. But in another sense it is by no means inevitable that we should read gaze direction in mentalistic terms—and, as was pointed out in chapter 5, biological development can go wrong in such a way that some people cannot read gaze in these terms.

Being able to interpret eye contact and eye direction in terms of a person's mental states is probably what gives us such a strong impression that the eyes are "windows to the soul." This is, of course, a common theme in literature. When we make eye contact, we usually also feel able to judge whether we have really "connected" with the other person. My guess is that what we are doing here is detecting if the other's attention is squarely on us or slightly away. Undivided, focused, dyadic eye contact gets interpreted as "He or she is fully attending to me." This may be one of the most powerful forms of behavioral evidence that we have achieved a "meeting of minds." Your mind (i.e., attention) is directed toward my mind (i.e., attention). The eyes are windows to the mind in the further sense that by observing the direction of someone's eyes we can identify the target of that person's desire or goal, since these correlate with the target of the gaze (Baron-Cohen, Campbell, et al., in press).

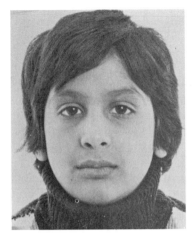
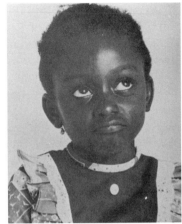

Figure 7.3
A pair of photographs from the "Which one is thinking?" test. Reproduced and
adapted from Baron-Cohen and Cross 1992.

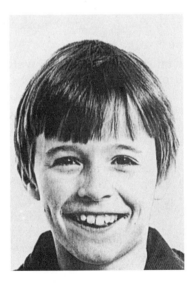
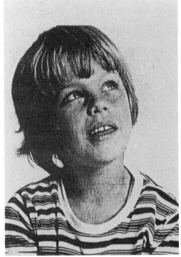

Figure 7.4
Another pair of photos from the "Which one is thinking?" test. Reproduced and
adapted from Baron-Cohen and Cross 1992.

When one considers eye direction in a static fashion (as in figure 7.2), the mapping of single mental states onto "frozen," clearly defined eye directions becomes quite clear. However, though we do sometimes observe someone holding a stare or a "fixed look" at an object (or at us) for an extended period of time, gaze shifts are more usually part of a fluid, rapidly changing motion. The eyes are constantly moving balls. In real life, gaze direction shifts rapidly and in partially unpredictable sequences. It is here that I want to push the analogy of gaze and language. It seems to me to be at least plausible that, if each constituent part of gaze is read as a meaningful unit (e.g., "He wants x"), then complex gaze sequences, despite being silent and unspoken, may have the richer meanings that such "syntax" can provide. In a real sense, there may be a language of the eyes.

The Language of the Eyes

The idea of a language of the eyes is, of course, not new. In the seventeenth century the poet George Herbert wrote (in *Jacula Prudentum*) that "the eyes have one language everywhere." In the nineteenth century the essayist Ralph Waldo Emerson echoed this in *Conduct of Life: Behavior*:

> The eyes of men converse as much as their tongues, with the advantage that the ocular dialect needs no dictionary, but is understood all the world over. . . . An eye can threaten like a loaded and leveled gun, or can insult like hissing or kicking; or in its altered mood, by beams of kindness, it can make the heart dance with joy.

The idea of a language of the eyes goes back at least as far as the Roman poet Ovid (43 B.C.–10 A.D.), who wrote "There are often voice and words in a silent look" (*Ars Amatoria*, book 1, line 574). In my own work, I have been influenced by Tapio Nummenmaa, who wrote an interesting monograph entitled *The Language of the Face* (1964). Nummenmaa systematically tested whether recognition of various emotions in photographs was more dependent on the eye region or on the mouth region of the face. He did this by cutting up the photos into different regions.

His studies showed that, whereas the "simple emotions" (e.g., happy and sad) could be recognized from either the mouth or the eye region, recognizing the "complex" emotions (surprise, cruelty, combinations of surprise and anger, etc.) required information from the eye region. Figure 7.5 shows Nummenmaa's "eye-region" stimuli; figure 7.6 shows his "mouth-region" stimuli.

What Range of Meanings Do the Eyes Convey?
It is interesting to attempt to extend Nummenmaa's notion of a "language of the face" by considering the specific notion of a language of the eyes. It appears that early in the second year of life infants can read some emotional states (e.g., fear and joy) from eye direction and facial expression (Sorce et al. 1985). And it is my guess that adults have an enormous vocabulary of eye meanings. Unsystematic evidence for this can be found in poetry,[8] which often tries to describe perceptions of the emotions and attitudes of others. Shakespeare, for example, talked of "pity-pleading eyes" (*The Rape of Lucrece*, stanza 81). He also noted aggression in the eyes:

> Thou tell'st me there is **murder** in my eye;
> 'Tis pretty, sure, and very probable,
> That eyes, that are the frail'st and softest things,
> Who shut their coward gates on atomies,
> Should be call'd tyrants, butchers, murderers!
> (*As You Like It*, act 3, scene 5)

(Here, as above, I have used boldface to emphasize the intentional and emotional states.) Shakespeare's description of fear conveyed by the eyes is apparent in the following:

> Alack! There lies more **peril** in thine eye,
> Than twenty of their swords
> (*Romeo and Juliet*, act 2, scene 2)

Byron echoes this theme of the eyes' conveying emotion:

> Her eye (I'm very fond of handsome eyes)
> Was large and dark, suppressing half its fire

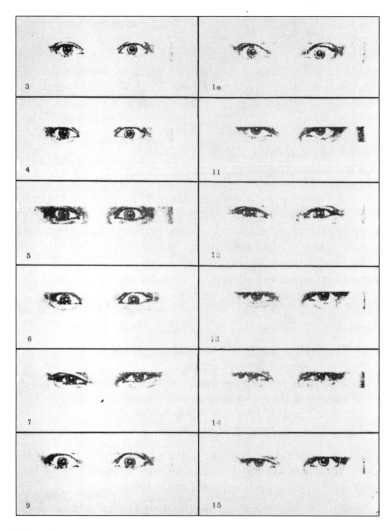

Figure 7.5
The eye regions of twelve faces. Reproduced from Nummenmaa 1964.

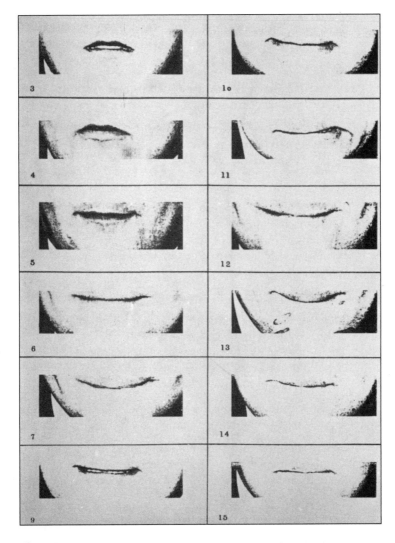

Figure 7.6
The mouth regions of the same twelve faces as in figure 7.4. Reproduced from
Nummenmaa 1964.

> Until she spoke, then through its soft disguise
> Flash'd an expression more of **pride** than **ire**,
> And **love** than either . . .
> (*Don Juan*, canto i, stanza 60)

Many writers have been impressed with the beauty of the eyes. Here is Shakespeare again:

> For where is any author in the world
> Teaches such beauty as a woman's eye?
> (*Love's Labour's Lost*, act iv, scene 3)

And:

> If I could write the beauty of your eyes,
> And in fresh numbers say all your graces,
> The age to come would say, "This poet lies;
> Such heavenly touches ne'er touch'd earthly faces
> (Sonnets, no. 17)

Shelley was equally struck by the beauty of the eyes:

> Thine eyes are like the deep, blue, boundless heaven,
> Contracted to two circles underneath
> Their long, fine lashes; dark, far, measureless,
> Orb within orb, and line through line inwoven
> (*Prometheus Unbound*, act 2, scene 1)

Shelley also commented on the widely held idea that love is transmitted through the eyes:

> Sweet, silent rhetoric of **persuading** eyes,
> Dumb eloquence, whose power doth move the blood
> More than the words or wisdom of the wise
> (*Complaint of Rosamond*, stanza 19)

And he noted the prolonged eye contact of lovers:

> Think ye by gazing on each other's eyes
> To multiply your lovely selves?
> (*Prometheus Unbound*, act 3, scene 4)

Shakespeare pointed out the same thing:

A lover's eyes will gaze an eagle blind
(*Love's Labour's Lost*, act 4, scene 3)

Were never four such lamps together mix'd
("Venus and Adonis")

Donne's poem "The Ecstasy" describes eye contact in quite sexual terms:

Our eye-beams twisted and did thread
Our eyes, upon one double string;
So to, engraft our hands, as yet
Was all the means to make us one,
And pictures in our eyes to get
Was all our propagation.

Ovid, too, noticed how sexual intent could be read from the eyes:

Non oculi tacuere tui
(Your eyes were not silent)
(*Amores*, book 2, elegy 5)

In "That the Eye Bewrayeth," the sixteenth-century poet Sir Thomas Wyatt brings out another commonly held view—that a person's real motives are revealed by the eyes rather than by words:

For it is said by man expert
That the eye is **traitor** of the heart.

A similar idea is inherent in the ancient and universal "evil eye" phenomenon: "An evil mind, it seems likely, must have an evil eye." (Gifford 1958, p. 3)

The eyes' simpler communicative function of conveying a request was noted by the eighteenth-century poet Samuel Rogers:

And her dark eyes—how eloquent!
Ask what they would, 'twas granted
("Jacqueline," part 1).

Finally, Shelley noted that negative emotions can be read in the eyes:

Two starry eyes, hung in the **gloom of thought**
("Alastor," line 490)

These passages from literature hint at the richness of the language of the eyes. The strong fascination with the eyes, across cultures and ages derives, I suggest, from the basic evolutionary mechanisms described in chapter 4. Clearly the poets are constructing cultural meanings here, and these might well vary from age to age or from culture to culture; however, the fascination with the eyes and the attraction to them that run through these passages seem to be universal.[9]

In table 7.1 I have attempted to compile a more complete list of mental states that can be conveyed by the eyes, a number of

Table 7.1
Some mentalistic interpretations of the eyes, listed as mental states and their semantic opposites.

i	Troubled*/Unconcerned
ii	Caring*/Uncaring
iii	Certain*/Uncertain
iv	Reflective/Unreflective
v	Serious*/Playful
vi	Sad*/Happy
vii	Near-focus/Faraway-focus
viii	Noticing you/Not noticing you
ix	Dominant/Submissive
x	Friendly/Hostile
xi	Interested/Disinterested
xii	Desire/Hate
xiii	Trust/Distrust
xiv	Alertness/Fatigue
xv	Scheming/Sincere
xvi	Surprise/Knowing
xvii	Anger/Forgiveness

*depicted in figure 7.7

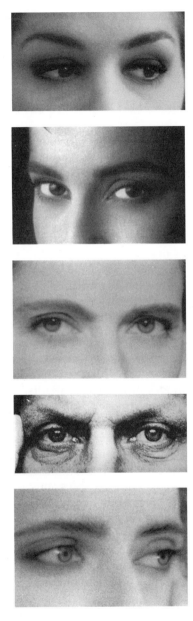

Figure 7.7
Five examples of eyes expressing mental states. (See table 7.1.) (These are fragments of photos originally published in various magazines. The identities of the faces are no longer traceable, nor are the sources.)

which we have tested empirically (Baron-Cohen 1995d). Some of these overlap with the meanings already mentioned. I have listed them as semantic opposites in order to suggest that mental states lie on continua and that both poles of each continuum can be read in the eyes, possibly with degrees of these mental states being discriminable between these poles. Finally, some of the items in this list describe "speech acts" that the eyes can convey, rather than mental states per se.

Each of the various meanings of the eyes must be a function of a very small number of variables: the size of the pupils, the position of the eyelids, the position of the pupil relative to the sclera, the speed of the eyes' motion, the "focus" of the eyes, and the shape of the eyebrows. It remains for further work to sort out which of the mental states listed above are reliably discriminated from the eye region alone, whether the physical configurations depicting these mental states overlap or are distinct, and whether other mental states can be read.

The English language offers a fairly extensive vocabulary for describing the eyes, and obviously this must map onto the meanings the eyes can convey. Consider the following passage:

> That men do discriminate, or try to discriminate, the postures and movements of the eyes of another person is strongly suggested by the number of words used in ordinary speech to distinguish modes of looking. Variants of the verb "to look" include **stare**, **watch**, **peer**, **glance**, **peep**, **glare**, **glower**, **contemplate**, and **scan**. Adverbial modifiers of the verb are frequent. A person can be said to look **directly**, or **askance**, **overtly**, or **covertly**, **boldly**, or **bashfully**, **sternly**, or **mildly**, **critically**, or **kindly**, or even **unseeingly**. Among the many idiomatic expressions or metaphors are: **he caught my eye**, or **held my eye**, or **looked me up and down**, or **his eyes dropped**, or **flickered**, or **his gaze wandered**. A person may either **cast an eye on**, or **fasten his eyes on**, or **look down his nose at**. He may **steal a glance**, give a **sidelong glance**, or a **guarded glance**, or have a **discerning glance**, **a piercing glance**, or

a **fixed stare**. He may also give one a **sly look**, an **open look**, or a **black look**. These examples suggest that the task of judging expressions of emotion entails a separate and distinct problem, that of judging what might be called the expression of **attention**. (Gibson and Pick 1962, pp. 386–387)

Other commonly used descriptions of the eyes that I have collected include the following:

an unswerving stare
frenzied eyes
mad eyes
burning eyes
looking daggers
a faraway look
glazed eyes
a knowing look
playful eyes
making eyes

I don't know if the English language is particularly rich in its vocabulary for eye meanings, but I suspect that equivalent sets of descriptions exist in other languages.

The belief in the "evil eye," mentioned above, certainly exists in many languages:

In all languages this universal belief has received a special name. The ancient Romans called the eye with magic power for harm *oculus fascinus*, the fascinating eye, and the ancient Greeks used the word *baskania*. The *oculus fascinus* was known to the Hebrews as *ayn-hara*, and among the Syrians as *aina-bisa*.

To the modern Italians the evil eye is the *mal occhio*. In Naples, where the belief is still intense, natives speak of *la jettatura*. In Tuscany this ocular power is called *affascinamento* or *mal d'occhio*. In Corsica it is the *innochiatura*. Today in France it is *mauvais oeil*; in Spain *mal de ojo*; in Germany

böse Blick; in Holland *booze blik*; in Poland *zte oko*; in
Norway *skjoertunge*; in Denmark *et ondt oje*; in Scotland
cronachadt; in Ireland *droch-shuil*; in Persia *aghashi*; in
Armenia *paterak*; among the southern Slavs *urok*; in Greece
avascama; in Hungary *szemveres*; in Morocco *l'ain*; in
Ethiopia *ayenat*; in southern India *drishtidosham*. (Gifford
1958, p. 6)

Social psychology, of course, has an extensive literature on
eye contact. Argyle (1972) reviews experiments showing how
eye contact is synchronized with starting or finishing to speak
(Kendon 1967)—the speaker making initial eye contact just after
starting, but then looking away as if to signal that his or her
intention not to be interrupted. A speaker may also look away so
as not to be distracted by the listener's face from the complexities of speech production and utterance planning. A speaker
typically looks back at a listener just before finishing his or her
message, presumably to check the listener's attention and reac-
tion to the message.

Proximity and duration of eye contact clearly also vary with
the relationship between the individuals. Lovers spend an inor-
dinate length of time making close eye contact (Rubin 1970;
Thayer and Schiff 1977), as one can observe by looking at cou-
ples in a restaurant. In one imaginative study (Ellsworth 1975),
researchers riding motorcycles stared at other drivers while
stopped at traffic lights and observed that stared-at motorists
moved off more rapidly when the lights turned green than those
not stared at. And—consistent with the tendency to interpret
gaze as threatening, sometimes with minimal justification—one
study of football hooligans found that a single glance from a
member of the opposing group can start a fight, preceded by
cries of "He looked at me!" (Marsh, Hare, and Rosser 1978, cited
in Argyle 1990).[10]

The Psychophysics of EDD
Presumably, when EDD detects eyes it is actually detecting the
strong contrast between the white of the sclera and the dark of

the iris and the pupil. Contrast sensitivity is, of course, a general property of the visual system, but the notion of an EDD suggests that it is more than just a contrast detector. In all likelihood, the contrast has to have a particular eye-like circular form, and there have to be two of them for the system to fire most strongly. It is worth noting that it in humans the sclera remains white throughout life, so that the contrast remains clearly detectable—possibly in order to emphasize the mentalistic and communicative significance that the eyes have throughout an individual's life. In other primates the sclera may become dark, possibly to minimize another animal's ability to detect that the primate is looking at it (Perrett and Mistlin 1990).

The poets are right, I think, in noting that we find the eyes not only important but also beautiful. Their beauty is enhanced by emphasizing their dark-light contrast, for instance with the use of eye liner, or eye shadow, and my guess is that such devices serve to exaggerate the features to which EDD responds: shape, contrast, and movement.

The adult human's preoccupation with the eyes, I want to argue, has a long history. It starts when, as very young infants, we become bewitched by adults playing "peekaboo" with us—a game in which, as the adult covers and uncovers his or her eyes, the infant watches the adult's eye region in an almost mesmerized state. The infant typically smiles or laughs when the adult's eyes reappear. Bruner (1983) cited such games as instances of early, routinized social interaction. My guess is that we adults are aware, at some level, not only of how important eyes are to us but also of how infants seem attracted to them. They watch us blinking, they imitate this (Meltzoff 1990), and they turn to follow our direction of gaze (from 9 months or so). Our eyes give them a clue as to our target of attention; they also provide a clue to our interpretation of events, since our gaze is usually embedded within an emotional facial expression (of interest, pleasure, fear, surprise, disgust, anger, etc.).

Interest in the eyes goes back to pre-human times. As I write this sentence, I am looking at the bare, white-washed stone walls of an old house in Provence. A lizard has just appeared on the wall from behind the shutters. I look up at him and he freezes; I turn my gaze away and he scurries off into the shadows of the wooden beams of the ceiling. The eye-direction detector has come a long way from this ancient reptile to the human adult, but its essence is quite obviously the same. Have I convinced you that EDD is an extraordinary piece of our neurocognitive architecture?

Chapter 8

Mindreading: Back to the Future

> If I may add a comment of my own, I am led to impute to [chimpanzees] some measure of imputation to others of first-hand experience. . . . (Lloyd Morgan 1930, cited in Whiten and Perner 1991)

In this final chapter I want to look back in evolutionary terms by looking at which parts of the mindreading system can be found in non-human animals alive today. I also want to anticipate some interesting research questions and controversies that lie ahead, some of which stem from the theory I have proposed in this book.

Mindreading in Non-Humans

Can the Chimpanzee Mindread?
As the epigraph above reveals, Cannon Lloyd Morgan—a pioneering primatologist known for his rigorous prescription that theorists adhere to the principle of parsimony in interpreting evidence—reached the conclusion that chimpanzees were indeed aware of the inner states of others. Was his conclusion justified?

David Premack and Guy Woodruff, the two primatologists who in the 1970s were responsible for reopening the question of the mindreading abilities of non-human primates, concluded from their investigations that "the ape could only be a mentalist . . . he is not intelligent enough to be a behaviorist" (Premack and Woodruff 1978). Were these scientists right?

Premack and Woodruff reached their conclusion after inviting their chimpanzee Sarah to carry out a series of tasks that measure mindreading. In one such test, Sarah had to watch a video of a person trying to do something, and the film was frozen before the action was completed. Sarah was required to choose the picture depicting the solution to the actor's problem. For instance, the videotape showed the actor inside a cage, jumping up and down, apparently trying to reach some bananas that were out of reach. Because Sarah passed this task with ease (e.g., choosing the picture of the actor climbing up onto a chair), Premack and Woodruff concluded that Sarah was capable of mindreading, at least at the level of being able to attribute volitional states, such as goals and desires, to the actor. Sarah "recognized the videotape as a problem, understood the actor's purpose, and chose alternatives compatible with that purpose" (ibid., p. 515). If this was true, then in the model of mindreading that I presented above the chimpanzee could be said to have an ID.

In the commentaries that followed Premack and Woodruff's original study, several people challenged their conclusion (Bennett 1978; Dennett 1978b). Bennett suggested that the chimp could have performed the task mentioned above without attributing volitional states to the actor by simply choosing what comes next in a schematic action sequence. In reply, Premack argued that this interpretation of the task is unlikely, although this alternative possibility needs to be firmly ruled out in the case of the ape. Premack's own conclusions are as follows:

> The chimpanzee has passed tests suggesting that it attributes states of mind to the other one. These states, however, are either motivations (e.g., he **intends** to get the banana . . .), or perceptual (e.g., he **sees** which container is baited . . .). Decisive evidence for the attribution of informational states [such as **belief**] is still lacking. (Premack and Dasser 1991, p. 265)

Whether Premack is right or not, there seems to be considerable agreement today on the view, first proposed by Jolly (1966) and Humphrey (1984), that the intelligence of the higher primates is an adaptation for solving the problems posed by the social world (see chapter 2 above). The picture arising from field observations suggests, according to Whiten and Perner (1991, p. 3),

> a primate who has a sophisticated knowledge of the individual characteristics and propensities of others in the group, and the network of social relationships existing between them; a flexible capacity to form cooperative alliances with some, so outmaneuvering others in competition for resources; and a considerable repertoire of tactics for social manipulation, ranging from deception to reciprocal helping. . . . Primates are thus portrayed as little "Machiavellians," several of their strategies being just those advocated by the pioneering power theorist's advice to sixteenth century princes and politicians.

However, saying that many non-human primates may be aware of who is allied to who, of who has power, and of how to behave in order to maintain or change the balance of power in social groups, is not the same as saying that they understand that they and others have mental states. As Byrne and Whiten (ibid., p. 128) note:

> A claim that primates were in any sense "mindreading" would have to rest on evidence of higher order intentionality . . . Level Two evidence of deception. Here, deception itself must be intended and the agent must attribute intentions to other animals; we have to be sure that 'animal1 wants (animal2 to believe X)', where X is false.

The latter criterion is, I think, appropriate as a measure of whether an animal possesses a theory-of-mind mechanism; however, even an animal that showed no signs of deception would not be precluded from possessing one or more of the other components of the mindreading system. But on the question of deception, although there are lots of instances in which the behavior of monkeys and apes looks pretty smart (and these are collected from diverse fieldwork records by Byrne and Whiten), these reviewers conclude, after going through each of the anecdotes using the criterion above, that the idea that monkeys or apes are mindreaders still requires a verdict of "not proven." Indeed, they say, "in many cases an account in terms of only instrumental conditioning seemed perfectly plausible" (ibid., p. 128).

In sum: If Premack is right, and on the basis of the evidence I reviewed in chapter 7, then in terms of the mindreading model, both ID and EDD are present and functional in many primates, enabling them to interpret another animal's behavior in terms of the other animal's goals and desires and in terms of whether the other animal can see them. However, the evidence that either SAM or ToMM is present in these primates is still thin. It may be that SAM is a part of the chimpanzee's cognitive architecture, and observations of the sort made by the primatologist Franz de Waal would certainly lead to this view:

> Another point in common with [the human and] the chimpanzee is the critical role of eye contact. Among the apes it is a prerequisite for reconciliation. It is as if chimpanzees do not trust the other's intentions without a look in the eyes. In the same way, we do not consider a conflict settled with people who turn their eyes to the ceiling or the floor each time we look in their direction. (De Waal 1989, p. 43)

It is necessary to repeat my cautionary note from chapter 7 about the importance of being sensitive to species-specific differences in the meaning of behavior. In particular, recent experiments by Daniel Povinelli and Timothy Eddy (in press) throw doubt on the idea that SAM is present in chimpanzees, since chimps appear to request objects from a human keeper irrespective of whether the keeper is looking at them or away, suggesting they may not recognize the significance of a gaze directed away. That is, Povinelli and Eddy found that young chimps would selectively make requests of the trainer who was facing forward when given a choice between this trainer and one who was facing in the opposite direction—and they performed in this "correct" fashion from trial 1. In contrast, they did not selectively make requests of the trainer whose eyes were directed forward when given the choice between this trainer and one whose face was directed forward but whose eyes were directed away. Povinelli and Eddy conclude:

> Our findings provide little evidence that young chimpanzees understand seeing as a mental event . . . even as [they] automatically attend to and follow the visual gaze of others, they simultaneously appear oblivious to the attentional significance of that gaze. Thus, young chimpanzees learn rules about visual perception, but these rules do not necessarily incorporate the notion that "seeing" is 'about' something.

What about other species of ape? I want to focus on a species for which a special case has been made: the bonobo, or the pygmy chimpanzee. Discovered in the early part of this century, these apes have been described as our closest living relatives, sharing with us intelligence, a varied sexual life (including face-to-face mating), and a degree of bipedalism.

My reason for paying special attention to the bonobo here is that, according to de Waal's descriptions (which contain a useful summary of their behavior and habitat), this may be the only monkey or ape species to *play with its perception* of the world, at least with any seriousness (de Waal 1992). De Waal describes a game he observed which looks a lot like the human child's game Blind Man's Buff: one bonobo covered its eyes with some material and then stumbled around on its climbing frame in the zoo, attempting to balance at heights of about 5 meters from the ground, blindfolded! One interpretation of this behavior is that bonobos are aware of being able to see or not see, and find it interesting to manipulate what they can see in terms of what they then discover about their own abilities. Of course, this is only an isolated anecdote, and more systematic research would be needed, but it may be that this ability to apparently reflect on the act of perceiving is present in bonobos as well as in humans, and that it is therefore only valid to ascribe SAM to both species. The relevant experiments are beginning to be carried out (Povinelli, Parks, and Novak 1991; Povinelli and Eddy, in press),[1] but much still needs to be done.

Another strategy for inferring whether non-human primates are mindreaders, even to degrees, is to look at their communication. Pinker (1994, pp. 340–341) summarizes the findings from studies of chimpanzees that have been taught "sign language"':

> . . . the chimps rarely make statements that comment on interesting objects or actions; virtually all of their signs are demands for something they want, usually food or tickling. I cannot help but think of a moment with my two-year-old niece Eva that captures how different are the minds of child and chimp. One night the family was driving on an expressway, and when the adult conversation died down, a tiny voice from the back seat said "Pink." I followed her gaze, and on the horizon several miles away I could make out a pink neon sign. She was commenting on its color, just for the sake of commenting on its color.

Pinker calls such comments "declaratives," to contrast them with the requests that (he notes) characterize the spontaneous communication of the chimps, which consists mostly of "imperatives." If one takes declaratives to be a way of sharing attention to an event or an object, then the presence of declaratives is an indirect indicator that an organism possesses a shared-attention mechanism. One bonobo studied by Sue Savage Rumbaugh appeared to use graphic signs for functions other than requesting, though at best it did so on only 4 percent of trials (Pinker 1994, p. 341).

Which Components of the Mindreading System Do Various Organisms Have?

What can we conclude about the phylogeny and the ontogeny of the mindreading system? Table 8.1 is an attempt to summarize the ideas from this chapter and the earlier ones in relation to ten different populations, including three age groups of biologically normal humans, five types of human psychopathology, and two varieties of non-human animals. These populations were chosen on the basis of existing evidence in order to highlight how different combinations of the components of the mindreading system might exist.

Table 8.1
Presence (+) or absence (−) of each of the components of the mindreading system in ten populations.

	ID	EDD	SAM	ToMM
(A) Biologically normal humans				
(i) >4 years	+	+	+	+
(ii) 9–18 months	+	+	+	−
(iii) <9 months	+	+	−	−
(B) Humans with psychopathologies				
(iv) children and adults with congenital blindness	+	−	+	+
(v) children with autism (subgroup A)	+	+	−	−
(vi) children with autism (subgroup B)	+	+	+	−
(vii) children and adults with mental handicap, mental age > 4 years (age-equivalent)	+	+	+	+
(viii) children and adults with specific language disorder, mental age >4 years (age-equivalent)	+	+	+	+
(C) Non-human animals				
(ix) higher primates	+	+	+?	−
(x) many "lower" animals	−	+	−	−

I hope the reader will forgive me for the simplification that table 8.1 creates. It allows me to make the point that genetic differences between species and biological differences that involve some kinds of neuropathology within a species, as well as developmental differences within humans, may lead to some of the components of the mindreading system being unavailable to some organisms, in different combinations.

Note that, according to my theory, in order for ToMM to be present in an organism, SAM must also be present (see populations i, iv, vii, and viii). This is because the theory proposes that ToMM is triggered by SAM. However, note also that the possession of SAM in no way entails the development of ToMM (see populations ii, vi, and ix). Clearly, other populations should be considered in relation to this phylogenetic, ontogenetic, and neuropathological classification. In view of the claims I made in chapter 6,[2] one such group is children with orbito-frontal lesions acquired early in development. Assessing different species will also be an important challenge.

Current and Future Issues in the Study of Mindreading

In this final section, I turn to a variety of issues which are currently producing interesting and important debates in the field, and which will need to be resolved in the future research if any progress is to be made in this area.

The Cognitive Basis of ToMM in Humans

A variety of debates concerning the cognitive basis of this mechanism are underway. For example, Perner (1993) holds that mature mindreading requires a capacity for metarepresentation, which entails (among other things) the capacity to understand misrepresentation. For Perner, this capacity requires an across-the-board cognitive change rather than a domain-specific change. His is thus an anti-modular view. This view needs to be tested further. Hughes and Russell (1993) hold that an appreciation of another's belief states requires a mature executive function, defined as a system (thought to be located in the frontal cortex) that allows the mind to disengage from current input, and formulate plans, prior to action. For Russell, then, a ToMM may be secondary to a sense of agency, which itself depends on the executive system. (A variation on this position is seen in work by Sally Ozonoff (in press), who holds that the executive system and ToMM may be independent, frontal systems.) Both I and Alan Leslie also subscribe to this independence position (Baron-Cohen and Ring 1994; Leslie and Roth 1993). Russell's idea that ToMM is secondary to executive function and agency is likely to run into difficulties in explaining why individuals in so many other clinical groups have executive-function problems and yet have developed ToMM. (These syndromes are as varied as obsessive-compulsive disorder, hyperactivity, and conduct disorder.) However, there may be important interactions between executive function and ToMM.

Others also take issue with the modularity thesis of ToMM. For example, Gopnik and Wellman (1992, 1994) attribute the normal 4-year-old's competence at understanding opaque informational states such as beliefs to a theory change, brought about (much as occurs in science) when the evidence not fitting a current theory becomes insupportable. This idea reminds us that the child's theory of mind is working on input (data) all the time. It will be crucial to specify what types of input might cause a theory change of the sort that Wellman and Gopnik propose.

An alternative to the notion of ToMM, Brothers and Ring (1992) posit the existence of a "social module" rather than a mindreading system as discrete as the one described in the present book. As I mentioned in chapter 6, to my mind a social module is too broad a characterization. If a social module exists, then the mindreading system must be one part of this, but it is likely that the mindreading system is an independent part of it. This is because the evidence from the neuropsychology of autism suggests that it is possible for an individual to be impaired in this system without having a global deficit in social understanding (Baron-Cohen 1991a).

More evidence for the modularity of the mindreading system, and especially for the modularity of ToMM, comes from studies which have contrasted understanding of mental and non-mental representations by children with autism. Whereas a large number of experiments have shown that such children are impaired in understanding beliefs that do not match the world, they are able to understand such non-mental representations as photographs (Leekam and Perner 1991; Leslie and Thaiss 1992), drawings (Charman and Baron-Cohen 1992), and models (Charman and Baron-Cohen 1994b), even when these do not match the world. This suggests that it is the special nature of mental representations that poses difficulty for children with autism. Although this is grist for the modularity theorist's mill, some critical experiments still remain to be done: for example, beliefs and photographs differ in terms of their visibility, and it may be that the former are hard to understand because of this property. To clarify the modularity question here will require well-controlled experiments.

The Role of First-Person Experience
This is an important topic that has so far received relatively little consideration. It is clear that human adults not only attribute mental states to others but also experience having mental states. Presumably the same is true of young children and of non-human animals. Human infants experience wanting something, or expecting something, or noticing something, or thinking that an object is located somewhere, yet the role of such first-person experience in the construction or the development of the mind-reading system is not clear. If it is necessary, in what way does it play its part? Is it the case, for example, that we are first aware of our own mental states, and that we then extend this experience to others by analogy, merely "simulating" being them when we want to take into account what they might be thinking or feeling? This was certainly the view originally advocated by Humphrey (1984). However, it is hard to understand why, if this first-person experience is so important, children with autism fail to develop a normal mindreading system, since they presumably experience mental states themselves. An alternative possibility, consistent with Humphrey's position, is that we not only have these mental states but we are able to introspect on them, and that it is the knowledge that is a product of such introspection that we then ascribe to others. This position seems plausible, since this would then predict that both introspection and ascription of mental states to others would be hard for children with autism. There is some evidence that this is the case.

On the Relation between Language and Mindreading
A good case has been made by Noam Chomsky that there is a "language faculty"—what Steve Pinker (1994) calls a "language instinct." Pinker goes a step further than Chomsky in arguing persuasively that this is the result of natural selection. The question naturally arises as to the relation—if any—between a lan-

guage faculty and the mindreading system. Surprisingly, this is not addressed in Pinker's excellent book on the nature and evolution of language. I will deal with this big topic only briefly here, in order to highlight some issues.

It is clear that, in such evolutionary discussions, we are dealing with speculative argument. Despite this, it is worth laying out some of the possible scenarios. Did language evolve first, and mindreading second? Or was it the other way around? Might there have been an inevitable order to these events, based on one system's being necessary for the other? Or did the two faculties evolve quasi-independently, that is, to solve independent problems, but then mutually scaffold the other?

Reading Pinker 1994, one might initially think that mindreading comes "for free" with the language faculty: "We can shape events in each other's brains with exquisite precision. . . . Simply by making noises with our mouths, we can reliably cause precise new combinations of ideas to arise in each other's minds." (p. 15) In the same vein, Pinker argues that the benefit of a standard vocabulary in any given language community is that it makes it possible to "convey a concept from mind to mind virtually instantaneously" (p. 84). Pinker is absolutely right that this is one key use of language—to inform each other, to influence each other's thoughts. But would we do this if we weren't already mindreaders? I think not. To see why not, consider a person who has an intact language faculty but who cannot mindread (autism arguably being such a case). Such a person would be able to reply in perfectly well formed sentences when asked a question like "Where do you live?" but would be unable to engage in social dialogue—normal communication.

Pinker is surely right in saying "Chances are that if you find two or more people together anywhere on earth, they will soon be exchanging words" (ibid., p. 17). However, I would argue that this drive to inform, to exchange information, to persuade, or to find out about the other person's thoughts is principally based on mindreading, and that mindreading is enabled by the language faculty. But by itself, unless it is linked up to the mindreading system, the language faculty may hardly be used—at least, not socially.

To summarize: Why would people bother to talk if they weren't also mindreaders, interested in informing others and learning about the information others have? And people don't need to have a whole lot of syntax to mindread, it appears, at least at the simple levels of wanting to share information with others; a 14-month-old toddler who points at the moon and says "Moon!" while exchanging glances with you, and smiling, is hardly using much syntax. But the fact that the toddler checks to see if you have turned to look at what she is pointing at shows that she was not using the word or the gesture just for herself. Arguably, she was intending to direct your attentional state to an object or event that she herself found interesting. As Pinker says (1994, p. 267), most normally developing babies like to shmooze. But the drive to shmooze is not linguistic per se—it lies in the development of the mindreading system.

At higher levels in human development, it has also been argued that many communicative acts, such as irony and sarcasm, would be impossible without a developed mindreading system (Baron-Cohen 1988; Sperber and Wilson 1986; Happé 1994) that can recognize the speaker's intention behind the words actually spoken. Pinker (1994, pp. 229–230) acknowledges the relation between language and mindreading in the following way: "Human communication is not just a transfer of information like two fax machines connected by a wire; it is a series of alternating displays of behavior by sensitive, scheming, second-guessing, social animals."

The limitation of a language faculty without an accompanying mindreading system suggests that mindreading may have preceded language in evolution. However, that mindreading may have benefited from the existence of a language faculty, both phylogenetically and ontogenetically, is also quite plausible. Studies of this relationship have hardly begun.

What Are the Necessary Precursors in the Development of Mindreading?
This is a question that is currently attracting a lot of attention. Thus, while I and others (Mundy, Sigman, and Kasari 1993;

Tantam 1992; Baron-Cohen 1989e, 1991d) have stressed the necessity of joint attention (which in my own theory is driven by SAM) for the development of ToMM, others have stressed completely independent processes as necessary precursors. For example, Meltzoff and Gopnik (1993) propose that the infant's capacity for imitation is what is crucial, on the basis that this is what gives the infant the understanding of what another person might be experiencing when the other person is performing the same action (or making the same facial expression) as the infant. This is a fascinating proposal, and one suggested by a number of other theorists too (Rogers and Pennington 1991; Hay, Stimson, and Castle 1991; Whiten 1991).[3] However, the fact that evidence for an imitation deficit in autism is inconsistent (Charman and Baron-Cohen 1994c) means that the processes involved may be considerably more complex than simply "imitation causes theory of mind."

Hobson (1993b) favors a different precursor: the infant's capacity for emotional responsivity in the first months of life. Trevarthen (1979) proposes another, related process: what might be called the infant's "social motivation," or the drive to communicate. It is too early to give an answer to the important question of which of these proposals is right, since the relevant longitudinal research studies have not yet been completed (see Charman et al., unpublished). One possibility is that some of these "candidate precursors" are actually irrelevant to the development of mindreading—that one can become a competent mindreader without one or another of these. Another possibility is that one or a combination of these processes are indeed necessary precursors for mindreading. Answering these questions will be an important step for the field.

A Comparison of Various Models of the Mindreading System
The development of models of the mindreading system is still in its infancy, but I want to highlight some of the differences among the models that have been proposed, so that it will become clearer where critical tests need to be directed in future research. My own model of the mindreading system was presented in chapter

4. For comparison I have selected two alternative models, one proposed by Leslie (1994) and one by Premack (1993). (Leslie's model of the mindreading system was also referred to in chapter 4.)

Leslie, in effect, proposes a module that identifies whether something that moves does so as a result of internal or external forces (a "mechanics" module—ToBy). He then proposes ToMM, which he subdivides into $ToMM_1$ and $ToMM_2$; the former identifies actions that Agents are performing on objects, while the latter computes the attitudes Agents are holding toward propositions. $ToMM_1$ also identifies what an Agent is perceiving. Premack's model also proposes three modules: module 1 identifies goals or intentions, module 2 represents the value and power of an intentional act ("hard" or "soft," "prosocial" or "antisocial," "coercive" or "non-coercive," etc.), and module 3 identifies three classes of mental state (perception, desire, and belief).

It is not difficult to see commonalities between my own model and those of Leslie and Premack. The similarities are really in terms of the "first" and "final" modules in each system, at least as these are listed in table 8.2. That is, each of the three models includes a "first" module for identifying goal-directed agency, and each includes a "final" module for identifying the full range of mental states an Agent might hold. At least one reason for the similarities between my model and Premack's is that ID is very similar to the system that Premack described in 1990, which influenced my own thinking on this considerably. Similarly, there is an overlap with the "final" module in my system and Leslie's because I have largely borrowed Leslie's concept of ToMM, unchanged.

My model differs from the other two in that I have included a separate module (EDD) for detecting the eyes of an organism (because I think this is one way to capture the special preference different animals show for looking at the eyes) and a separate module (SAM) for checking whether the self and another agent are attending to the same thing. I have two reasons for suggesting that SAM must be separate. First, children with autism and

Table 8.2
Overlaps and differences among three models of mindreading.

Mental state	Model		
	Baron-Cohen	Leslie[a]	Premack
Desire	ID	ToBy	Module 1
Goal (refer)	ID	ToMM$_1$	Module 1
Value/Power[b]	—	—	Module 2
See, look	EDD	ToMM$_1$	ToM
Joint attention	SAM	—	—
Intend, pretend, believe, etc.	ToMM	ToMM$_2$	ToM

a. These modules have these functions in part, though they also have other functions not listed here.
b. This is a social relation rather than a mental state.

congenital blindness appear to be mirror opposites as concerns this (the former are impaired in this, while the latter are not—see table 8.1). Second, SAM seems to enter normal develop significantly earlier than the "final" module. Future research will have to test to what extent the distinctions each of these models makes are justified.

Individual Differences in "Empathy"
Some individuals are so tuned in to their own viewpoints that they are largely insensitive to the viewpoints of others. Such individuals can understand another's viewpoint when it is pointed out, but may not have considered it spontaneously or intuitively themselves. Yet other people seem remarkably empathic, and with such people you feel you are really "connecting," or being understood. Currently we have no good way of measuring such individual differences.

Folklore has it that women are much better mindreaders than men. Is this true? If it is, is it the result of genetic differences? If so, do such differences also relate to the dramatic sex ratio in autism? (Autism is far more common in males than in females.)

It should in principle be the case that, just at we have tests of auditory memory or spatial ability that show the range of ability that can exist in the normal population in these processes, so we should be able to devise tests of mindreading which show up the differences between those who are highly adept mindreaders and those who can pass the current laboratory tests but who are quickly recognized by their peers in the real world to be "slow at reading social cues," or "socially a bit odd," or often "lacking in empathy."[4]

There is a further meaning to the term "empathy," which is sometimes confused with the term "sympathy." This further meaning relates to a primarily emotional response to the state of another. My model of the mindreading system says very little about the role of emotion. In part, this reflects my own view that we are still a long way from having a good theory of emotion. Clearly, future models of mindreading will need to give a full account of the role of emotion in this domain, since it is self-evident that human beings are not "cold" computational devices.

Varieties of Autism
You could be forgiven for thinking, from my account, that there are only two varieties of people with autism: those who have an impairment in both SAM and ToMM (group A in table 8.1) and those whose impairment is restricted to ToMM (group B). This is not what I want to argue. While I want to suggest that these two subgroups may be identified within the population of children and adults with autism, a variety of other subtypes are also likely to be found. For example, because autism is a developmental disorder, theories of autism need to be developmental too. With regard to my own theory, I suggest that individuals with autism may be delayed or deviant relative to the normal course of development of the mindreading system at any point (Baron-Cohen 1991c).

This means that there should be a subgroup of people with autism (probably adults) who have developed ToMM, at least at the 4-year-old level, and possibly at the 7-year-old level. Indeed, such individuals have been found both in the United Kingdom and in the United States (Bowler 1992; Ozonoff, Rogers, and Pennington 1991; Happé 1994). Such individuals, my theory predicts, should nevertheless have abnormalities of a more subtle kind in mindreading, perhaps simply because they developed their mindreading ability years later than is normally done. (This would be akin to identifying the difference between a native speaker of English and a person who learned English as a second language: the differences might remain very conspicuous, or they might be remarkably subtle.) Or it may be because the development of ToMM in their case was never complete. (I will describe one such individual at the close of this chapter.)

Equally, there will in all likelihood be individuals with autism who have not only some abnormality in the mindreading system but also other (independent) abnormalities. I have already mentioned individuals who suffer from both executive-system deficits and mindblindness. Indeed, it may be that this combination of deficits is widespread in autism, the former deficit producing the repetitive, rigid, inflexible behaviors associated with autism and the latter producing the social and communicative abnormalities that are its hallmarks. There is considerable support for such a view (Rutter and Bailey 1993; Ozonoff, in press; Leslie and Roth 1993; Baron-Cohen and Ring 1994). Notice, though, that problems in mindreading (such as in monitoring one's own desires and thoughts) could well interfere with planning abilities, and thus with executive function. The relationship between mindreading and executive function is by no means a straightforward one.

It is also likely that further subgroups of autism will involve impairments in other systems. For example, Frith (1989; see also Shah and Frith 1983, 1993) identifies one additional system—the drive for "central coherence"—which may be independent of both the mindreading system and the executive function system, and which in many individuals with autism may be impaired. The upshot is that we need to be careful about concluding that autism involves mindblindness and nothing else. My suggestion here is that autism involves mindblindness as a core deficit, but that other deficits may co-occur.

A related question is whether a capacity for shared attention is irreducible. In my model, the Shared Attention Mechanism is a "primitive" in the sense that it is not constructed out of other systems. However, some theorists, including Courchesne et al. (in press), have suggested that a capacity for joint attention may itself rest on a capacity for shifting attention flexibly, both socially and non-socially. Their proposal for autism is therefore that the joint-attention problems are secondary to attention-shifting deficits. This interesting idea should, in principle, be testable. Do patients with other conditions in which attention shifting is a problem (such as frontal-lobe disorder, hyperactivity, and cerebellar abnormalities) also show deficits in joint attention? If they do not, then the claim that joint attention depends on the same system as that involved in (non-social) attention shifting is weakened.

Early Detection of Autism
In recent years I have been attempting to apply the model of mindreading to the early diagnosis of autism. Regrettably, over the 50 years that have elapsed since autism was first recognized, the condition has continued to be diagnosed far too late. Thus, until the 1980s it was extremely common for autism to go unnoticed until the child reached school age, and in many cases it was misdiagnosed and only properly recognized much later in the person's life. Fortunately, cases of very late diagnosis or misdiagnosis are becoming rarer, but it is still the case that diagnosis much before 3 years of age is unusual.

My colleagues and I have been concerned to see whether autism can be identified at 18 months of age in children who are manifestly not developing an SAM and thus not showing even any incipient evidence of developing a ToMM. In a first study (Baron-Cohen, Allen, and Gillberg 1992), we looked at 18-month-olds who were at a higher genetic risk[5] for developing autism because of having a sibling with autism. We found that those toddlers who showed no joint attention at this age, and who showed no evidence of even simple pretend play, turned out to be undiagnosed cases of autism. In a second, much larger study (Baron-Cohen, Cox, Baird, Swettenham, Drew, Morgan,

Nightingale, and Charman 1994), we screened 16,000 toddlers in southeastern England, looking for the same pattern of missing behaviors. We found 17 such children who, on two assessments, showed no evidence of joint attention (the normal sign that SAM is intact) or pretend play (the normal sign that ToMM is beginning to develop). Again, the majority of these infants were diagnosed as having autism.

The fact that at 18 months each of the children with autism had a generalized deficit in shared attention (they neither produced the pointing gesture nor followed another person's gaze) is at least consistent with the notion that a deficit in SAM is fundamental to autism. This work is also important because it shows how the application of theory can be of practical value. If we can succeed in lowering the age of diagnosis, at the very least this will alleviate the unnecessary delays faced by the long-suffering families of such children. And it opens the possibility that intervention or treatment could be implemented at a much earlier point in the course of the disorder, with the hope of lessening the impact of mindblindness.

Can Mindblindness Be Overcome?

Some remarkable individuals with autism seem to overcome their mindblindness to some degree—certainly to the degree of being able to pass the trivial tests summarized in chapter 5. But does the fact that they no longer fail these tests (they can understand, for example, that people have beliefs and desires) mean that they are now normal mindreaders? Perhaps the best way of approaching this question is to look in detail at one astonishing individual with autism, Temple Grandin. She has a Ph.D. in agricultural science and works as a teacher and researcher at Colorado State University. She has written autobiographical books and articles as well as scientific articles on her research. Clearly, this kind of achievement would be almost impossible without the basic concepts of beliefs and desires. But is she a normal mindreader? Recently the neurologist Oliver Sacks visited her, at her home and at work, to find out.[6]

Temple's early development clearly had all the hallmarks of autism. For example, she started to engage in pretend play only at the age of 8 years, whereas a normal child does this as a toddler. At high school, Temple recalls, "I couldn't figure out what I was doing wrong. I had an odd lack of awareness that I was different. I thought the other kids were different. I could never figure out why I did not fit in." Sacks comments on this as follows:

> Something was going on between the other kids, something swift, subtle, constantly changing—an exchange of meanings, a negotiation, a swiftness of understanding so remarkable that sometimes she wondered if they were all telepathic. She is now aware of the existence of these social signals. She can infer them, she says, but she herself cannot perceive them, cannot participate in this magical communication directly, or conceive of the many-leveled, kaleidoscopic states of mind behind it.

This gives a hint that, while she is more socially aware as an adult, difficulties persist. Sacks investigated her adult abilities a little further:

> How did she respond to myths or to dramas? How much did they carry meaning for her? . . . She was bewildered, she said, by *Romeo and Juliet* ("I never knew what they were up to") and with *Hamlet* she got lost with the back-and-forth of the play. Though she ascribed these problems to "sequencing difficulties," they seemed to arise from her failure to empathize with the characters, to follow the intricate play of motive and intention. She said that she could understand "simple, strong, universal" emotions but was stumped by more complex emotions and the games people play. "Much of the time," she said, "I feel like an anthropologist on Mars."
>
> She was at pains to keep her own life simple, she said, and to make everything very clear and explicit. She had build up a vast library of experiences over the years, she

went on. They were like a library of videotapes, which she could play in her mind and inspect at any time—"videos" of how people behaved in different circumstances. She would play these over and over again, and learn, by degrees, to correlate what she saw, so that she could then predict how people in similar circumstances might act. She had complemented her experience by constant reading, including reading of trade journals and the *Wall Street Journal*—all of which enlarged her knowledge of the species. "It is a strictly logical process," she explained.

This gives us a clue as to how some successfully adapted individuals with autism may have managed to circumvent their mindblindness. Adopting what in chapter 1 I called the Contingency Stance, in place of her inability to use the Intentional Stance in the normal way, gives Temple Grandin some predictive power over the apparently unpredictable nature of human action. But does that mean she is cured? Sacks notes that Temple is still gullible, a target for all sorts of tricks and exploitation, as a result of "her failure to understand dissembling and pretense," and that she acts "without diffidence or embarrassment (emotions unknown to her)." Such clues suggest that, although her achievement is remarkable in view of her early development, she still feels to some extent like "an anthropologist on Mars." Lacking the normal Intentional Stance, she must "'compute' others' feelings and intentions and states of mind, to try to make algorithmic, explicit, what for the rest of us is second nature." Note that her own description of feeling as if she is on an alien planet is actually an overstatement:

> One could not say that she was devoid of feeling or had a fundamental lack of sympathy. On the contrary, her sense of animals' moods and feelings was so strong that these almost took possession of her, overwhelmed her at times. She feels she can have sympathy for what is physical or physiological—for an animal's pain or terror—but lacks empathy for people's states of mind and perspectives. . . . At the level of the sensorimotor, the concrete, the unmedi-

ated, Temple is enormously sensitive. "I can tell if a human being is angry," she told me, "or if he is smiling."

Here, then, is an adult who has recovered from or overcome her mindblindness to a considerable extent. She can lecture, write books, live independently; however, in her own words, still cannot even play peekaboo with a baby, because she gets the timing all wrong. As for her understanding of language, she is

> still quite abnormal in her understanding of ordinary or social language—she still missed allusions, presupposi-tions, irony, metaphors, jokes—[but] found the language of science and technology a huge relief. It was much clear-er, much more explicit, with far less depending on unstat-ed assumptions. Technical language was as easy for her as social language was difficult, and now provided herself with an entry into science.

Technical language is, in a sense, more factual than "social lan-guage," which is riddled with figurative phrases that require one to compute the speaker's unspoken meaning or intention and which, clearly, is an area of persistent difficulty for Temple.

Finally, what of normal adult intimacy—in particular, sexu-ality? One might imagine that intimacy is intrinsically tied to mindreading ability. Indeed, the poets often liken the drive for sexual union to the drive for reaching into someone else's mind. Lovers feel a special closeness not just because of sexual inter-course but also because of deep mental intercourse—sharing secret wishes and fears and feeling as if you really know the other person's thoughts. Does Temple's limited mindreading ability allow her to enjoy such intimacy?

> No, she said. She was celibate. Nor had she ever dated. She found such interactions completely baffling, and too com-plex to deal with; she was never sure what was being said, or implied, or asked, or expected. She did not know, at such times, where people were coming from, or their assumptions, or presuppositions, or intentions. This was common with autistic people, she said, and one reason

why, though they had sexual feelings, they rarely succeeded in dating or having sexual relationships.

And her own explanation for these persisting difficulties? "She surmises that her mind is lacking some of the 'subjectivity,' the inwardness, that others seem to have."

For Temple Grandin, as for other adults with autism who I have met and who have made an astonishing adaptation to their disability, mindreading remains mysterious and confusing. They remain, to some extent, blind to the "language of the eyes."

Notes

Chapter 1

1. In philosophy of mind, the term "intentional" is used to refer to the whole set of terms that have intentionality—that is, the property of referring to or being directed at a propositional content. See Brentano 1874 and Dennett 1978a for further discussion.

2. See Hobson 1993a for a discussion of this idea in relation to autism.

3. Humphrey (1993) uses the term "mind-blindness" to refer to the condition of visual agnosia—when a person cannot recognize the objects he sees. The Berlin physiologist Hermann Munk (1878; cited in Benton 1991) was probably the first to coin the term "mindblindness," which he used to describe the condition resulting from destruction of the visual center in the occipital lobes in the dog. This also became known as visual agnosia. In their classic 1938 paper, Heinrich Kluver and Paul Bucy used a similar term—"psychic blindness"—to refer to experimental animals (usually monkeys) that visual agnosia as a result of bilateral temporal lobectomy. For Kluver and Bucy, this term was also intended to pertain to the social deficits these animals showed. I suggest the term is more appropriately applied to the condition of failing to recognize and understand mental states. Humphrey (1984, p. 40) hints that a monkey with "blindsight" (the condition of thinking that one cannot see), reared in isolation, would be "blind to the idea that another monkey can see. " This, I think, gets closer to my sense of mindblindness, although autism (as I hope will become apparent in chapter 5) is a real and far clearer example.

4. An example of Humphrey's simulation theory can been found on page 6 of his 1984 book. For a recent debate on simulation theory, see *Mind and Language* 6 (1992), nos. 1 and 2. For the opposite view, see Gopnik and Wellman 1994. I will return to simulation theory in chapter 8.

Chapter 2

1. Harlow and Harlow (1962) give a distressing description of what happens when, under scientific conditions, the attachment between an infant monkey and its adult caregiver is broken.

2. The term "module" here is borrowed from Fodor 1983. But whereas Fodor suggests a range of criteria for defining what will count as a module, these may not be appropriate for all modules. This will be elaborated in chapter 5. See Karmiloff-Smith 1992 and Baron-Cohen 1994b, 1995a for further discussion of the concept of modularity as applied to development.

3. In one sense, every problem can affect reproduction "distally"; however, Cosmides' idea is clear enough. Some problems have highly proximal effects on reproduction, and it is on such proximal mechanisms that we should focus.

4. In chapter 4 I will try to identify the mechanisms that could have evolved before or during the Pleistocene epoch to make us the skilled mindreaders that we are.

Chapter 3

1. I am well aware of the anthropomorphism inherent in talking of evolution "favoring" a solution. I hope the reader will forgive this occasional stylistic device, and will not interpret it literally.

2. This summary is taken from Baron-Cohen 1995b.

3. I am grateful to Alison Gopnik for the terms "brainoscope" and "mindoscope."

4. There must be huge variation among the folk psychologies of different cultures; however, their common basis is postulated to be the use of mental-state attribution in making sense of behavior.

5. See Baron-Cohen 1988 and Happé 1994 for further discussion.

Chapter 4

1. Premack's module is very similar to ID—indeed, it was the inspiration for it. See the following note, however.

2. Premack (1993) suggests that the input conditions for perception of GOAL be restricted to three kinds: Escape from confinement, Gravity-overcoming, and Seeking-to-make-contact. I would rather leave open the possibility of a far wider set of conditions.

3. However, one possibility is that ID may be a submodule of ToBy.

4. See also Phillips, Baron-Cohen, and Rutter 1992.

5. Perrett and Emery (1994) suggest that the mindreading system might also contain a "Direction of Attention Detector" (DAD). This mechanism would be amodal and would code attention from a range of cues: head direction, body posture, etc. I am not opposed to this suggestion. However, since ID already processes such information and codes it in terms of an Agent's goal, I am not yet persuaded that the addition of DAD contributes in an essential way. This is discussed further in Baron-Cohen 1994.

6. As will become clear in this section, my ideas about EDD coincide in many interesting respects with those proposed by Digby Tantam (1992), who argues

in detail for the idea that the human response to gaze involves a primitive mechanism. EDD is in some ways an attempt to specify the workings and limitations of such a mechanism.

7. On eye-like stimuli, see Blest 1957.

8. See also Spitz 1946.

9. Haith, Bergman, and Moore (1977) found that 7–11-week-old infants looked at the eyes approximately 10 times longer than at the mouth. Lasky and Klein (1979) found that 5-month-olds looked longer at faces that maintained eye contact than at faces that averted their gaze. Samuels (1985) and Ehrlich (1993) failed to observe any clear preference for eye contact over averted gaze in infants younger than this, but recently Vicera and Johnson (1994) did.

10. This term is also derived from the work of Bakeman and Adamson (1984) and Trevarthen (1979). Hobson (1984?, 1993a,b), too, makes use of the notion of "triangular" relations. In my theory, the term refers to a class of representation.

11. A triadic representation is not simply two dyadic representations in sequence, since this would not specify that at least one of the agents is aware that the other agent has perceived their perceiving the same object at the same time. To capture this, it seems to me, requires the embedding of two dyadic representations.

12. The idea of distinguishing EDD's dyadic functions and SAM's triadic functions echoes Tantam's (1992) clear distinction between eye contact and what he calls the "second-gaze response. "

13. See also Flavell, Green, and Flavell 1986 for a discussion of the development of visual perspective taking. Povinelli and Eddy (1994) argue that chimpanzees might show gaze monitoring without using SAM—that is, they may reorient to gaze shifts in another animal without any awareness that the other animal is attending to what they are attending to. Povinelli and Eddy therefore suggest that protodeclarative pointing may be a more clear-cut indicator of SAM, which never occurs in chimpanzees but which emerges at the same time as gaze monitoring in humans. See the whole debate in Baron-Cohen 1994b, in which the ideas discussed in the present chapter are thoroughly aired.

14. Baldwin (1991) has also reported 18-month-olds' ability to use eye direction to infer a person's intended referent.

15. Why the ability to represent the mental states of pretending should develop so much earlier than the abilities to represent false belief and deception is not yet clear.

16. See also Gopnik and Wellman 1992, 1994.

17. See *Mind and Language* 6 (1992), nos. 1 and 2.

18. To clarify further: SAM is necessary but not sufficient for ToMM to be triggered. See Baron-Cohen and Swettenham (in press) for additional options on whether SAM and ToMM really are independent mechanisms.

19. See also Trevarthen and Hubley 1978.

20. I admit to having put a lot into ToMM; its full development takes about 2 years. Future theorists may wish to add a further subdivision here, making five

mechanisms; however, for the moment, I find no good reason to subdivide this mechanism—at least, not on modular grounds (where modularity is defined in terms of the possibility of neuropathological dissociation).

Chapter 5

1. I am indebted to Hobson (1990) for bringing out the full importance of the comparison and the contrast between children with autism and congenital blindness.

2. The following account of autism is based on the information set out in Baron-Cohen and Bolton 1993, a book for parents. Excellent reviews of autism can be found in Frith 1989 and Wing 1976.

3. Much of this evidence is reviewed in Baron-Cohen 1990a and 1993. In the present chapter, I review this evidence in relation to each of the proposed mechanisms.

4. Children with autism can also recall their own previous desires (Baron-Cohen 1991c). This too suggests that ID is probably intact.

5. My own theorizing about SAM in autism owes much to Peter Mundy and Marian Sigman (who in 1984 first drew my attention to joint-attention deficits in autism and to the possibility that they were precursors of the "theory of mind" deficits in these children) and to Digby Tantam (whose 1992 theoretical paper suggested that the joint-attention problems in autism might be primary).

6. As was mentioned in chapter 4, this proposal owes much to Tantam's (1992, p. 85) claim that children with autism are impaired in "social attention" and specifically in the "second gaze response." The distinction that I make between SAM and EDD is intended to bring out the different mechanisms that are involved. See also Baron-Cohen 1994a.

7. For a full discussion of mental age in studies of autism, see Frith 1989. Frith herself builds on the approach developed by Hermelin and O'Connor (1970). Mental age is assessed by means of standardized tests, and it must be controlled for in studies of autism simply because a large proportion of children and adults with autism suffer not only from autism but also from an accompanying mental handicap. (This, by definition, gives a person a mental age lower than his or her chronological age.)

8. See, for example, Leekam and Perner 1991; Leslie and Thaiss 1992; Baron-Cohen 1989b; Reed and Peterson 1990. Each of these replications used a similar puppet story. Leslie and Frith (1988) replicated the study using real people instead of puppets, and Swettenham (1992) replicated it using a computer-graphic presentation of the same story.

9. A British candy, similar to American M&Ms.

10. See, for example, Rutter 1978. Two studies (Oswald and Ollendick 1989; Ozonoff, Pennington, and Rogers 1991) failed to replicate this pattern of results with the picture sequencing test. Oswald and Ollendick, however, did not report whether all 15 of the original stories were used, and this casts some

doubt on the validity of their replication. Ozonoff et al. did use the full set; they found that the children with autism performed significantly better on the physical causal stories, as Baron-Cohen, Leslie, and Frith (1986) found, but they did not replicate the finding of an autism-specific deficit in the mental-state condition (since in their study the control groups also performed poorly). It is clear that further studies are needed to establish the reliability of this paradigm.

11. Reed and Peterson (1990) went on to replicate these findings, this time including a mentally handicapped control group. They also found severe deficits in both understanding knowledge (23% of the autistic group passing) and belief (15% passing). This, again, suggests that knowledge is marginally easier than belief for children with autism but that understanding both of these mental states is impaired more severely in children with autism than in mentally handicapped children.

12. See for example Baron-Cohen 1987; Ungerer and Sigman 1981; Gould 1986; Charman and Baron-Cohen 1994a. There is some controversy here, however. For one thing, Lewis and Boucher (1988) found lower levels of functional play, though functional play in autism appears to be normal in other studies. Furthermore, they observed pretend play by children with autism under conditions of elicitation or instruction, whereas these children did not pretend in spontaneous play. This result is open to multiple interpretations (Baron-Cohen 1989c, 1990b; Boucher and Lewis 1990; Harris 1993). In addition, Kavanaugh and Harris (1994) report finding intact comprehension of the consequences of pretend actions in children with autism. However, it is not yet established that the method of Kavanaugh and Harris requires an understanding of pretense per se.

13. In his early studies, Hobson (1986a,b) found that subjects with autism performed significantly worse than control groups on emotion expression matching tasks. In later studies, these differences were not found when groups were matched on verbal mental age (Hobson, Ouston, and Lee 1988a,b, 1989; Tantam et al. 1989; Braverman et al. 1989; Prior, Dahlstrom, and Squires 1990; Ozonoff, Pennington, and Rogers 1990).

Emotion-recognition deficits are also found in a range of other clinical disorders, including schizophrenia (Cutting 1981; Novic, Luchins, and Perline 1984), mental handicap (Gray, Frazer, and Leuder 1983), child abuse (Camras, Grow, and Ribordy 1983), deafness (Odom, Blanton, and Laukhuf 1973), and prosopagnosia (De Kosky et al. 1980; Kurucz, Feldmar, and Werner 1979).

I have said nothing here about the experience of emotion in children with autism. Important though this must be, I have not included any relevant mechanism for this in the architecture of the mindreading system. However, there is suggestive evidence that an abnormality in empathy exists in autism (Yirmiya et al. 1992). This is without doubt an area in which more theoretical work needs to be done.

14. This result was replicated by Ozonoff , Pennington, and Rogers (1991).

15. This result too was replicated by Ozonoff, Pennington, and Rogers (1991).

Chapter 6

1. Single Photon Emission Computed Tomography.
2. Note, however, that SAM and ID, unlike EDD, are amodal. In this respect, they are likely to have a more complex brain basis.
3. In this study, the patients were tested for their ability to make the animate-inanimate distinction. This presumably overlaps with the agent/non-agent distinction, though the two are not identical.
4. Perhaps the earliest version of this hypothesis was proposed by Kleist (1931; cited in Benton 1992), who suggested that OFC-limbic regions formed a circuit dedicated to subserving "ego-functions. "
5. See Bishop 1992 for a review.
6. Brothers (1995) discusses not only the importance of the OFC, the STS, and the amygdala but also how such connections might mediate "hot" versus "cold" social cognition.

Chapter 7

1. The model of the mindreading system is presented as a target article in Baron-Cohen 1994b; that article is followed by various commentaries, to which specialist readers are directed.
2. Droscher 1971, p. 14. References for this paragraph can be found in that source.
3. Whether EDD fires when there is just one eye is an interesting question. My guess—that it fires most when it detects two eyes —has some support from Scaife 1976. In this respect it is probably responding to the "law of nature" that most predators have binocular rather than monocular vision. The phenomenon of two eyes (binocular vision) is presumably the product of a genetic law of nature, as is evident from the disorder known as cyclopism. This disorder gets its name from the Greek mythological figure Polyphemus, the Cyclops, with his single eye staring out from the center of his forehead. Cyclopism is a genetic mutation, attributable to radiation or poisons, in which a child or an animal is born with just one eye in the middle of the forehead. Cyclopism is also accompanied by other fetal abnormalities which leave the infant unable to survive more than a day after birth. Such genetic abnormalities reveal the genetic mechanisms controlling the development of two eyes, and these appear to be very old in evolutionary terms.
4. In this study the birds had both eye direction and head direction available as cues.
5. See Arduino and Gould 1984 for a review.
6. One possibility, raised by Povinelli and Eddy (in press), is that gaze monitoring in non-human primates, where it exists, is more reflexive than gaze monitoring in humans.
7. Anthropomorphism is clearly a danger here, but Leakey and Lewin's point is nevertheless clear, I think.

8. The source of the quotations in this section is Stevenson 1946.

9. I am indebted to Alison Gopnik, who reminded me that an ode to a lover's nose would be substantially more difficult to construct than one describing the lover's eyes. In view of the evolutionary argument pursued above, this comes as no surprise.

10. See Fehr and Exline 1978 for a full review of the social psychology of gaze, including a review of the factors that affect duration of gaze.

Chapter 8

1. Juan Carlos Gòmez also informed me that the gorilla called Muni (whom he describes in Whiten 1991) played with her perception in a way similar to the bonobo game of "blind man's buff. "

2. Valerie Stone and I are currently testing this claim.

3. Rogers and Pennington (1992) and Meltzoff and Gopnik (1993) review the relevant studies of imitation in autism, which are very relevant to the question of the precursor status of imitation in the development of ToMM. However, Charman and Baron-Cohen (1994c) report some data on autism that do not fit the imitation-as-precursor hypothesis easily. As the latter paper points out, the existing studies in this area of autism research suffer from having been carried out over a 30-year period, during which very different kinds of samples of children (in terms of mental age) were tested. This whole topic is therefore in need of a careful reexamination, in order to see which studies can be compared to which.

4. Wendy Phillips, Michael Rutter, and I are currently developing such tests.

5. See Folstein and Rutter 1988.

6. The following account of Temple Grandin is based solely on observations reported in *The New Yorker* (Sacks 1994).

References

Ackerley, S., and Benton, A. 1948. Report of a case of bilateral frontal lobe defect. *Association for Research in Nervous and Mental Disease* 27: 479–504.

Aggleton, J. 1985. A description of intra-amygdaloid connections in old world monkeys. *Experimental Brain Research* 57: 390–399.

Aggleton, J., Burton, M., and Passingham, R. 1980. Cortical and subcortical afferents to the amygdala of the rhesus monkey (*Macaca mulatta*). *Brain Research* 190: 347–368.

Alexander, M., Benson, D., and Stuss, D., 1989. Frontal lobes and language. *Brain and Language* 37: 656–659.

Altmann, S., ed., 1967. *Social Communication among Primates.* University of Chicago Press.

Amaral, D., and Price, J. 1984. Amygdalo-cortical projections in the monkey (*Macaca fascicularis*). *Journal of Comparative Neurology* 230: 465–496.

Arduino, P., and Gould, J. 1984. Is tonic immobility adaptive? *Animal Behavior* 32: 921–922.

Argyle, M. 1972. *The Psychology of Interpersonal Behavior.* Pelican. Reprint: Penguin, 1990.

Argyle, M., and Cook, M. 1976. *Gaze and Mutual Gaze.* Cambridge University Press.

Austin, J. 1962. *How to Do Things with Words.* Blackwell.

Avis, J., and Harris, P. 1991. Belief-desire reasoning among Baka children: Evidence for a universal conception of mind. *Child Development* 62: 460–467.

Bailey, A. 1993. The biology of autism. *Psychological Medicine* 23: 7–11.

Bakeman, R., and Adamson, L. 1984. Coordinating attention to people and objects in mother-infant and peer-infant interaction. *Child Development* 55: 1278–1289.

Baldwin, D. 1991. Infants' contribution to the achievement of joint reference. *Child Development* 62: 875–890.

Baldwin, D. 1994. Understanding the link between joint attention and language acquisition. In *Joint Attention: Its Origins and Role in Development*, ed. C. Moore and P. Dunham. Erlbaum.

Barbas, H. 1988. Anatomic organization of basoventral and mediodorsal visual recipient prefrontal regions in the rhesus monkey. *Journal of Comparative Neurology* 276: 313–342.

Baron-Cohen, S. 1987. Autism and symbolic play. *British Journal of Developmental Psychology* 5: 139–148.

Baron-Cohen, S. 1988. Social and pragmatic deficits in autism: Cognitive or affective? *Journal of Autism and Developmental Disorders* 18: 379–402.

Baron-Cohen, S. 1989a. Perceptual role-taking and protodeclarative pointing in autism. *British Journal of Developmental Psychology* 7: 113–127.

Baron-Cohen, S. 1989b. The autistic child's theory of mind: A case of specific developmental delay. *Journal of Child Psychology and Psychiatry* 30: 285–298.

Baron-Cohen, S. 1989c. The theory of mind hypothesis of autism: A reply to Boucher. *British Journal of Disorders of Communication* 24: 199–200.

Baron-Cohen, S. 1989d. Are autistic children behaviorists? An examination of their mental-physical and appearance-reality distinctions. *Journal of Autism and Developmental Disorders* 19: 579–600.

Baron-Cohen, S. 1989e. Joint attention deficits in autism: Towards a cognitive analysis. *Development and Psychopathology* 1: 185–189.

Baron-Cohen, S. 1990a. Autism: A specific cognitive disorder of "mind-blindness." *International Review of Psychiatry* 2: 79–88.

Baron-Cohen, S. 1990b. Instructed and elicited play in autism: A reply to Lewis and Boucher. *British Journal of Developmental Psychology* 8: 207.

Baron-Cohen, S. 1991a. The theory of mind deficit in autism: How specific is it? *British Journal of Developmental Psychology* 9: 301–314.

Baron-Cohen, S. 1991b. Do people with autism understand what causes emotion? *Child Development* 62: 385–395.

Baron-Cohen, S. 1991c. The development of a theory of mind in autism: Deviance and delay? *Psychiatric Clinics of North America* 14: 33–51.

Baron-Cohen, S. 1991d. Precursors to a theory of mind: Understanding attention in others. In *Natural Theories of Mind*, ed. A. Whiten. Blackwell.

Baron-Cohen, S. 1992. Out of sight or out of mind: Another look at deception in autism. *Journal of Child Psychology and Psychiatry* 33: 1141–1155.

Baron-Cohen, S. 1993. From attention-goal psychology to belief-desire psychology: The development of a theory of mind and its dysfunction. In *Understanding Other Minds: Perspectives from Autism*, ed. S. Baron-Cohen et al. Oxford University Press.

Baron-Cohen, S. 1994a. The Eye Direction Detector (EDD) and the Shared Attention Mechanism (SAM): Two cases for evolutionary psychology. In *The Role of Joint Attention in Development.*, ed. C. Moore and P. Dunham. Erlbaum.

Baron-Cohen, S. 1994b. How to build a baby that can read minds: Cognitive mechanisms in mindreading. *Cahiers de Psychologie Cognitive* 13: 513–552.

Baron-Cohen, S. 1995a. Modularity in developmental cognitive neuropsychology. In *Handbook of Mental Retardation and Development*, ed. J. Burack and E. Zigler. Cambridge University Press.

Baron-Cohen, S. 1995b. The development of a theory of mind: Where would we be without the Intentional Stance? In *Developmental Principles and Clinical Issues in Psychology and Child Psychiatry.*, ed. M. Rutter and D. Hay. Blackwell.

Baron-Cohen, S. 1995c. Face-processing and theory of mind: How do they inter-act in development and psychopathology? In *Manual of Developmental Psychopathology*, ed. D. Cicchetti and D. Cohen. Wiley.

Baron-Cohen, S. 1995d. The language of the eyes. Manuscript, University of Cambridge.

Baron-Cohen, S., and Bolton, P. 1993. *Autism: The Facts*. Oxford University Press.

Baron-Cohen, S., and Cross, P. 1992. Reading the eyes: Evidence for the role of perception in the development of a theory of mind. *Mind and Language* 6: 173–186.

Baron-Cohen, S., and Goodhart, F. 1994. The "seeing leads to knowing" deficit in autism: The Pratt and Bryant probe. *British Journal of Developmental Psychology* 12: 397–402.

Baron-Cohen, S., and Ring, H. 1994. A model of the mindreading system: Neuropsychological and neurobiological perspectives. In *Origins of an Understanding of Mind*, ed. P. Mitchell and C. Lewis. Erlbaum.

Baron-Cohen, S., and Swettenham, J. In press. The relationship between SAM and ToMM: The "lock and key" versus the "metamorphosis" hypotheses. In *Theories of Theories of Minds*, ed. P. Carruthers and P. Smith. Cambridge University Press.

Baron-Cohen, S., Allen, J., and Gillberg, C. 1992. Can autism be detected at 18 months? The needle, the haystack, and the CHAT. *British Journal of Psychiatry* 161: 839–843.

Baron-Cohen, S., Leslie, A., and Frith, U. 1985. Does the autistic child have a 'theory of mind'? *Cognition* 21: 37–46.

Baron-Cohen, S., Leslie, A., and Frith, U. 1986. Mechanical, behavioral and Intentional understanding of picture stories in autistic children. *British Journal of Developmental Psychology* 4: 113–125.

Baron-Cohen, S., Spitz, A., and Cross, P. 1993. Can children with autism recog-nize surprise? *Cognition and Emotion* 7: 507–516.

Baron-Cohen, S., Tager-Flusberg, H., and Cohen, D., eds. 1993. *Understanding Other Minds: Perspectives from Autism*. Oxford University Press.

Baron-Cohen, S., Campbell, R., Karmiloff-Smith, A., Grant, J., and Walker, J. Are children with autism blind to the mentalistic significance of the eyes? *British Journal of Developmental Psychology*, in press.

Baron-Cohen, S., Cox, A., Baird, G., Swettenham, J., Nightingale, N., Morgan, K., Drew, and Charman, T. 1994. Screening for autism versus language delay in a large population at 18 months of age: an investigation of the CHAT (Checklist for Autism in Toddlers). Unpublished manuscript, University of Cambridge.

Baron-Cohen, S., Ring, H., Moriarty, J., Shmitz, P., Costa, D., and Ell, P. Recognition of mental state terms: A clinical study of autism, and a functional neuroimaging study of normal adults. *British Journal of Psychiatry*, in press.

Bates, E. 1993. Invited lecture, MRC Cognitive Development Unit, London.

Bates, E., Benigni, L., Bretherton, I., Camaioni, L., and Volterra, V. 1979. Cognition and communication from 9–13 months: Correlational findings. In *The Emergence of Symbols: Cognition and Communication in Infancy*, ed. E. Bates. Academic Press.

Bauman, M., and Kemper, T. 1985. Histoanatomic observation of the brain in early infantile autism. *Neurology* 35: 866–874.

Bauman, M., and Kemper, T. 1988. Limbic and cerebellar abnormalities: consistent findings in infantile autism. *Journal of Neuropathology and Experimental Neurology* 47: 369.

Bayliss, G., Rolls, E., and Leonard, C. 1985. Selectivity between faces in the responses of a population of neurons in the cortex in the superior temporal sulcus of the monkey. *Brain Research* 342: 91–102.

Bennett, J. 1978. Some remarks about concepts. *Behavioral and Brain Sciences* 1: 557–560.

Benton, A. 191. The prefrontal region: Its early history. *In Frontal Lobe and Dysfunction*, ed. H. Levin et al. Oxford University Press.

Bishop, D. 1992. Autism and frontal-limbic functions. *Journal of Child Psychology and Psychiatry* 34: 279–294.

Blest, A. 1957. The function of eyespot patterns in the Lepidoptera. *Behavior* 11: 209–256.

Boucher, J., and Lewis, V. 1990. Guessing or creating? A reply to Baron-Cohen. *British Journal of Developmental Psychology* 8: 205–206.

Bowlby, J. 1969. *Attachment*. Hogarth.

Bowler, D. M. 1992. Theory of Mind in Asperger Syndrome. *Journal of Child Psychology and Psychiatry* 33: 877–893.

Braverman, M., Fein, D., Lucci, D., and Waterhouse, L. 1989. Affect comprehension in children with pervasive developmental disorders. *Journal of Autism and Developmental Disorders* 19: 301–316.

Brentano, F. von 1874. *Psychology from an empirical standpoint*. ed. O. Kraus. Routledge and Kegan Paul, 1970.

Brodmann, K. 1925. *Vergleichende localisationlehre der Grosshirnrinde*, second edition. Leipzig: Barth.

Brothers, L. 1990. The social brain: A project for integrating primate behavior and neurophysiology in a new domain. *Concepts in NeuroScience* 1: 27–51.

Brothers, L. 1995. The neurophysiology of the perception of intentions by primates. In *The Cognitive Neurosciences*, ed. M. Gazzaniga. MIT Press.

Brothers, L., and Ring, B. 1992. A neuroethological framework for the representation of minds. *Journal of Cognitive NeuroScience* 4: 107–118.

Brothers, L., Ring, B., and Kling, A. 1990. Responses of neurons in the macaque amygdala to complex social stimuli. *Behavioral Brain Research* 41: 199–213.

Brown, D. 1991. *Human Universals*. McGraw-Hill.

Bruce, C., Desimone, R., and Gross, C. 1981. Visual properties of neurones in a polysensory area in superior temporal sulcus of the macaque. *Journal of Neurophysiology* 46: 369–384.

Bruner, J. 1983. *Child's Talk: Learning to Use Language*. Oxford University Press.

Burghardt, G. 1990. Cognitive ethology and critical anthropomorphism: A snake with two heads and hog-nosed snakes that play dead. In *Cognitive Ethology: The Minds of Other Animals*, ed. C. Ristau. Erlbaum.

Butter, C., and Snyder, D. 1972. Alterations in aversive and aggressive behaviors following orbital frontal lesions in rhesus monkeys. *Acta Neurobiologica*, 32: 525–565.

Butterworth, G. 1991. The ontogeny and phylogeny of joint visual attention. In *Natural Theories of Mind*, ed. A. Whiten. Blackwell.

Byrne, R., and Whiten, A 1988. *Machiavellian Intelligence: Social Expertise and the Evolution of Intellect in Monkeys, Apes, and Humans*. Oxford University Press.

Byrne, R., and Whiten, A. 1991. Computation and mindreading in primate tactical deception. In *Natural Theories of Mind*, ed. A. Whiten. Blackwell.

Campbell, R., Heywood, C., Cowey, A., Regard, M., and Landis, T. 1990. Sensitivity to eye gaze in prosopagnosic patients and monkeys with superior temporal sulcus ablation. *Neuropsychologia* 28: 1123–1142.

Camras, L., Grow, G., and Ribordy, S. C. 1983. Recognition of emotional expression by abused children. *Journal of Child Psychology and Psychiatry* 12: 325–328.

Chance, M. 1956. Social structure of a colony of *Macaca mulatta*. *British Journal of Animal Behavior* 4: 1–13.

Chance, M. 1967. The interpretation of some agonistic postures: The role of "cut-off" acts and postures. *Symposium of the Zoological Society of London* 8: 71–89.

Charman, T., and Baron-Cohen, S. 1992. Understanding beliefs and drawings: A further test of the metarepresentation theory of autism. *Journal of Child Psychology and Psychiatry* 33: 1105–1112.

Charman, T., and Baron-Cohen, S. 1994a. Pretend play in autism: Object substitution and generativity. Unpublished manuscript, University College London.

Charman, T., and Baron-Cohen, S. 1994b. Understanding models, photos, and beliefs: A further test of the modularity thesis of metarepresentation. Unpublished manuscript, University College London.

Charman, T., and Baron-Cohen, S. 1994c. Another look at imitation in autism. *Development and Psychopathology* 6: 403–413.

Charman, T., Baron-Cohen, S., Swettenham, J., Cox, T., and Baird, G. Testing 4 candidate precursors of theory of mind. Unpublished manuscript, University College London.

Cheney, D., and Seyfarth, R. 1990. *How Monkeys See the World*. University of Chicago Press.

Churchland, P. 1981. Eliminative materialism and propositional attitudes *Journal of Philosophy* 78: 647–90.

Cosmides, L., Tooby, J., and Barkow, J. 1992. Introduction: Evolutionary psychology and conceptual integration. In *The Adapted Mind*, ed. J. Barkow et al. Oxford University Press.

Courchesne, E., Townsend, J., Akshoomoff, N., Saitoh, O., Yeung-Courchesne, R., Lincoln, A., James, H., Haas, R., Schreiman, L. and Lau, L. Impairment in shifting attention in autistic and cerebellar patients. *Behavioral Neuroscience*, in press.

Curcio, F. 1978. Sensorimotor functioning and communication in mute autistic children. *Journal of Autism and Childhood Schizophrenia* 8: 281–292.

Cutting, J. 1981. Judgement of emotional expression in schizophrenics. *British Journal of Psychiatry* 139: 1–6.

Damasio, A., Tranel, D., and Damasio, H. 1990. Individuals with sociopathic behavior caused by frontal lobe damage fail to respond autonomically to socially charged stimuli. *Behavioral Brain Research* 14: 81–94.

Darwin, C. 1872. *The Expression of Emotions in Man and Animals*. University of Chicago Press, 1965.

Dasser, V., Ulbaek, I., and Premack, D. 1989. The perception of intention. *Science* 243:, 365–367.

De Bruin, J. 1990. Social behavior and the primate cortex. In *Progress in Brain Research*, volume 85, ed. H. Uylings et al. Elsevier.

De Kosky, S., Heilman, K., Bowers, M., and Valenstein, E. 1980. Recognition and discrimination of emotional faces and pictures. *Brain and Language* 9: 206–214.

De Long, G. 1978. A neuropsychologic interpretation of infantile autism. In *Autism: A Reappraisal of Concepts and Treatment*, ed. M. Rutter and E. Schopler. Plenum.

De Waal, F. 1992. *Peacemaking among Primates*. Penguin.

Dennett, D. 1978a. *Brainstorms: Philosophical Essays on Mind and Psychology*. Harvester.

Dennett, D. 1978b. Beliefs about beliefs. *Behavior and Brain Sciences* 4: 568–570.

Dennett, D. 1987. *The Intentional Stance*. MIT Press.

Droscher, V. 1971. *The Magic of the Senses: New Discoveries in Animal Perception*. Panther Books.

Dunbar, R. 1993. Coevolution of neocortical size, group size, and language in humans. *Behavioral and Brain Sciences* 16: 681–735.

Dunn, J., and Dale, N. 1984. I a daddy: 2 year olds' collaboration in joint pretence with sibling and with mother. In *Symbolic Play. The Development of Social Understanding*, ed. L. Bretherton. Academic Press.

Ellsworth, P. 1975. Direct gaze as a social stimulus: The example of aggression. In *Nonverbal Communication and Aggression*, ed. P. Pliner et al. Plenum.

Erhlich, S. 1993. Infant perception of gaze-direction. In Proceedings of the 60th Anniversary Meeting of the Society for Research in Child Development.

Eslinger, P., and Damasio, A. 1985. Severe disturbance of higher cognition after bilateral frontal lobe ablation: Patient EVR. *Neurology* 35: 1731–1741.

Fairburn System of Visual References. 1978. Fairburn.

Fehr, B., and Exline, R. 1978. Social visual interaction: A conceptual and literature review. In *Nonverbal Behavior and Communication*. second edition, ed. A. Siegman and S. Feldstein. Erlbaum.

Flavell, J., Green, F., and Flavell, E. 1986. Development of knowledge about the appearance-reality distinction. *Monographs of the Society for Research in Child Development* 51.

Fodor, J. 1983. *The Modularity of Mind*. MIT Press.

Folstein, S., and Rutter, M. 1988. Autism: Familial aggregation and genetic implications. *Journal of Autism and Developmental Disorders* 18: 3–30.

Fraiberg, S. 1977. *Insights from the Blind*. Souvenir.

Frith, C. In press. Brain mechanisms for "having a theory of mind." In *The Psychopharmacology of Social Communication and Its Disorders*, ed. J. Deakin. Oxford University Press.

Frith, U. 1989. *Autism: Explaining the Enigma*. Blackwell.

Gale, A., Lucas, B., Nissim, R., and Harpham, B. 1972. Some EEG correlates of face to face contact. *British Journal of Social and Clinical Psychology* 11: 326–332.

Galin, D., and Ornstein, R. 1974. Individual differences in cognitive style. 1. Reflective eye movements. *Neuropsychologica*, 12: 367–376.

Gallup, G., Cummings, W., and Nash, R. 1972. The experimenter as an independent variable in studies of animal hypnosis in chickens (*Gallus gallus*). *Animal Behavior* 20: 166–169.

Gergely, G., Nádasdy, Z., Csibra, G., and Bíró, S. Taking the Intentional Stance at 12 Months of Age. *Cognition* , in press.

Gibson, J., and Pick, A. 1962. Perception of another person's looking behavior. *American Journal of Psychology* 76: 386394.

Gifford, E. 1958. *The Evil Eye: Studies in the Folklore of Vision*. Macmillan.

Gòmez, J. C. 1991. Visual behavior as a window for reading the minds of others in primates. In *Natural Theories of Mind.*, ed. A. Whiten. Blackwell.

Goodhart, F., and Baron-Cohen 1993. How many ways can children with autism make the point? *First Language* 13: 225–233.

Gopnik, A. 1993. Mindblindness. Unpublished essay, University of California, Berkeley.

Gopnik, A., and Wellman, H. 1992. Why the child's theory of mind really is a theory. *Mind and Language* 7: 145–171.

Gopnik, A., and Wellman, H. 1994. The theory theory. In *Mapping the Mind: Domain Specificity in Cognition and Culture*, ed. L. Hirschfeld and S. Gelman. Cambridge University Press.

Gould, J. 1986. The Lowe and Costello Symbolic Play Test in socially impaired children. *Journal of Autism and Developmental Disorders* 16: 199–213.

Gray, J., Frazer, W., and Leuder, I. 1983. Recognition of emotion from facial expression in mental handicap. *British Journal of Psychiatry* 142: 566–571.

Grice, H. P. 1967. Logic and conversation. Reprinted in *Syntax and Semantics: Speech Acts*, ed. R. Cole and J. Morgan. Academic Press, 1975.

Gur, R., Gur, R., and Harris, L. 1975. Cerebral activation, as measured by subjects' lateral eye movements, is influenced by experimenter location. *Neuropsychologia* 13: 35–44.

Hainline, L. 1978. Developmental changes in visual scanning of face and non-face patterns by infants. *Journal of Experimental Child Psychology* 25: 90–115.

Haith, M., Bergman, T., and Moore, M. 1977. Eye contact and face scanning in early infancy. *Science* 198: 865–855.

Hall, K., and Devore, I. 1965. Baboon social behavior. In *Primate Behavior*, ed. I. Devore. Holt, Rinehart and Winston.

Happé, F. 1994. Communicative competence and theory of mind in autism: A test of Relevance Theory. *Cognition* 48: 101–119.

Harlow, H., and Harlow, M. 1962. Social deprivation in monkeys. *Scientific American* 207: no. 2: 136.

Harris, P. 1993. Pretending and planning. In *Understanding Other Minds: Perspectives from Autism*, ed. S. Baron-Cohen et al. Oxford University Press.

Harris, P., Johnson, C., Hutton, D., Andrews, G., and Cooke, T. 1989. Young children's theory of mind and emotion. *Cognition and Emotion* 3: 379–400.

Hauser, S., DeLong, G., and Rosman, N. 1975. Pneumographic findings in the infantile autism syndrome. *Brain* 98: 667–688.

Hay, D., Stimson, C., and Castle, J. 1991. A meeting of minds in infancy: imitation and desire. In *Children's Theories of Mind*, ed. D. Frye and C. Moore. Erlbaum.

Heider, F., and Simmel, M. 1944. An experimental study of apparent behavior. *American Journal of Psychology* 57: 243–259.

Hermelin, B., and O'Connor, N. 1970. *Psychological Experiments with Autistic Children.* Pergamon.

Heywood, C., and Cowey, A. 1991. The role of the "face-cell" area in the discrimination and recognition of faces by monkeys. *Philosophical Transactions of the Royal Society of London* B 335: 1–128.

Hietanen, J., and Perrett, D. 1991. A role of expectation in visual and tactile processing within temporal cortex. In *Brain Mechanisms of Perception and Memory: From Neuron to Behavior*, ed. T. Ono et al. Oxford University Press.

Hobson, R. P. 1984. Early childhood autism and the question of egocentrism. *Journal of Autism and Developmental Disorders* 14: 85–104.

Hobson, R. P. 1986a. The autistic child's appraisal of expressions of emotion. *Journal of Child Psychology and Psychiatry* 27: 321–342.

Hobson, R. P. 1986b. The autistic child's appraisal of expressions of emotion: A further study. *Journal of Child Psychology and Psychiatry* 27: 671–680.

Hobson, R. P. 1990. On acquiring knowledge about people and the capacity to pretend: Response to Leslie [1987]. *Psychological Review* 97: 114–121.

Hobson, R. P. 1993a. *Autism and the Development of Mind.* Erlbaum.

Hobson, R. P. 1993b. Understanding persons: The role of affect. In *Understanding Other Minds: Perspectives from Autism*, ed. S. Baron-Cohen et al. Oxford University Press.

Hobson, R. P., Ouston, J., and Lee, A. 1988a. What's in a face? The case of autism. *British Journal of Developmental Psychology* 79: 441–453.

Hobson, R. P., Ouston, J., and Lee, A. 1988b. Emotion recognition in autism: Coordinating faces and voices. *Psychological Medicine* 18: 911–923.

Hobson, R. P., Ouston, J., and Lee, T. 1989. Naming emotion in faces and voices: Abilities and disabilities in autism and mental retardation. *British Journal of Developmental Psychology* 7: 237–250.

Holroyd, S., and Baron-Cohen, S. 1993. Brief Report: How far can people with autism go in developing a theory of mind? *Journal of Autism and Developmental Disorders* 23: 379–386.

Horwitz, B., Rumsey, J., Grady, C., and Rapoport, S. 1988. The cerebral metabolic landscape in autism: Intercorrelations of regional glucose utilization. *Archives of Neurology* 45: 749–755.

Hughes, C., and Russell, J. 1993. Autistic children's difficulty with mental disengagement from an object: Its implications for theories of autism. *Developmental Psychology* 29: 498–510.

Humphrey, N. 1984. *Consciousness Regained*. Oxford University Press.

Humphrey, N. 1986. *The Inner Eye*. Faber and Faber.

Humphrey, N. 1993. *A History of the Mind*. Vintage.

Jolly, A. 1966. Lemur social behavior and primate intelligence. *Science* 153: 501–506.

Kaczmarek, B. 1984. Neurolinguistic analysis of verbal utterances in patients with focal lesions of frontal lobes. *Brain and Language* 21: 52–58.

Kanner, L. 1943. Autistic disturbance of affective contact. *Nervous Child*, 2: 217–250. Reprinted in Kanner, *Childhood Psychosis: Initial Studies and New Insights* (Wiley, 1973).

Karmiloff-Smith, A. 1992. *Beyond Modularity: A Developmental Perspective on Cognitive Science*. MIT Press.

Karmiloff-Smith, A., Grant, J., Bellugi, U., and Baron-Cohen, S. Is there a social module? Face-processing and theory of mind in William's Syndrome and autism. *Journal of Cognitive Neuroscience.*, in press.

Kavanaugh, R., and Harris, P. 1994. Imagining the outcome of pretend transformations: Assessing the competence of normal and autistic children. *Developmental Psychology* (in press).

Keating, C., and Keating, E. 1982. Visual scan patterns of rhesus monkeys viewing faces. *Perception* 11: 211–219.

Kendon, A. 1967. Some functions of gaze direction in social interaction. *Acta Psychologica*, 28: 1–47.

Kling, A., and Brothers, L. 1992. The amygdala and social behavior. In *Neurobiological Aspects of Emotion, Memory, and Mental Dysfunction*, ed. J. Aggleton. Wiley-Liss.

Kluver, H., and Bucy, P. 1938. An analysis of certain effects of bilateral temporal lobectomy in the rhesus monkey, with special reference to "psychic blindness." *Journal of Psychology* 5: 33–54.

Kurucz, J., Feldmar, G., and Werner, W. 1979. Prosopo-affective agnosia associated with chronic organic brain syndrome. *Journal of the American Geriatrics Society*, 27: 91–95.

Landau, B., and Gleitman, L. 1985. *Language and Experience: Evidence from the Blind Child*. Harvard University Press.

Lasky, R., and Klein, R. 1979. The reactions of 5 month old infants to eye contact of the mother and a stranger. *Merrill-Palmer Quarterly* 25: 163–170.

Leakey, R., and Lewin, R. 1992. *Origins Reconsidered*. Little, Brown.

Leekam, S., and Perner, J. 1991. Does the autistic child have a metarepresentational deficit? *Cognition* 40: 203–218.

Leekam, S., Baron-Cohen, S., Perrett, D., Milders, M., and Brown, S. 1993. Eye-direction detection: A dissociation between geometric and joint-attention skills in autism. Unpublished manuscript, Institute of Social Psychology, University of Kent.

Lempers, J. D., Flavell, E. R., and Flavell, J. H. 1977. The development in very young children of tacit knowledge concerning visual perception. *Genetic Psychology Monographs* 95: 3–53.

Leonard, C., Rolls, E., Wilson, F., and Bayliss, G. 1985. Neurons in the amygdala of the monkey with responses selective for faces. *Behavior and Brain Research* 15: 159–176.

Leslie, A. 1987. Pretence and representation: The origins of "theory of mind." *Psychological Review* 94: 412–426.

Leslie, A. 1991. The theory of mind impairment in autism: Evidence for a modular mechanism of development? In *Natural Theories of Mind*, ed. A. Whiten. Blackwell.

Leslie, A. 1994. ToMM, ToBy, and Agency: Core architecture and domain specificity. In *Mapping the Mind: Domain Specificity in Cognition and Culture*, ed. L. Hirschfeld and S. Gelman. Cambridge University Press.

Leslie, A., and Frith, U. 1988. Autistic children's understanding of seeing, knowing, and believing. *British Journal of Developmental Psychology* 6: 315–324.

Leslie, A., and Roth, D. 1993. What can autism teach us about metarepresentation? In *Understanding Other Minds: Perspectives from Autism*, ed. S. Baron-Cohen et al. Oxford University Press.

Leslie, A., and Thaiss, L. 1992. Domain specificity in conceptual development: Evidence from autism. *Cognition* 43: 225–251.

Lewin, R. 1992. *Human Evolution*. Blackwell.

Lewis, V., and Boucher, J. 1988. Spontaneous, instructed and elicited play in relatively able autistic children. *British Journal of Developmental Psychology* 6: 325–339.

Lloyd-Morgan, C. 1930. *The Animal Mind*. Edward Arnold.

Loveland, K., and Landry, S. 1986. Joint attention and language in autism and developmental language delay. *Journal of Autism and Developmental Disorders* 16: 335–349.

Mandler, J. 1992. How to build a baby, II: Prelinguistic primitives. *Psychological Review* 99: 587–604.

Marsh, P., Harre, R., and Rosser, E. 1978. *The Rules of Disorder*. Routledge and Kegan Paul.

Maurer, D. 1985. Infants' perception of facedness. In *Social Perception in Infants*, ed. T. Field and N. Fox. Ablex.

Maurer, D. 1993. Neonatal synaesthesia: Implications for the processing of speech and faces. In *Developmental Neurocognition: Speech and Face Processing in the First Year of Life*, ed. B. de Boysson-Bardies et al. Kluwer.

McBride, G., King, M., and James, J. 1965. Social proximity effects on galvanic skin responses in adult humans. *Journal of Psychology* 61: 153–157.

Meltzoff, A. 1990. Towards a developmental cognitive science: The implications of cross-modal matching and imitation for the development of representation and memory in infancy. *Annals of the New York Academy of Sciences* 608: 1–37.

Meltzoff, A., and Gopnik, A. 1993. The role of imitation in understanding persons and developing a theory of mind. In *Understanding Other Minds: Perspectives from Autism*, ed. S. Baron-Cohen et al. Oxford University Press.

Mendelsohn, M., Haith, M., and Goldman-Rakic, P. 1982. Face scanning and responsiveness to social cues in infant monkeys. *Developmental Psychology* 18: 222–228.

Menzel, E., and Halperin, S. 1975. Purposive behavior as a basis for objective communication between chimpanzees. *Science* 189: 652–654.

Mundy, P., Sigman, M., and Kasari, C. 1993. Theory of mind and joint attention deficits in autism. In *Understanding Other Minds: Perspectives from Autism*, ed. S. Baron-Cohen et al. Oxford University Press.

Mundy, P., Sigman, M., Ungerer, J., and Sherman, T. 1986. Defining the social deficits in autism: The contribution of nonverbal communication measures. *Journal of Child Psychology and Psychiatry* 27: 657–669.

Nagel, T. 1974. What is it like to be a bat? *Philosophical Review* October. Reprinted in *The Mind's I*, ed. D. Hofstadter and D. Dennett. Harvester, 1981.

Nakamura, K., Mikami, A., and Kubota, K. 1992. Activity of single neurons in the monkey amygdala during performance of a visual discrimination task. *Journal of Neurophysiology* 67: 1447–1463.

Nichols, K., and Champness, B. 1971. Eye gaze and the GSR. *Journal of Experimental Social Psychology* 7: 623–626.

Novic, J., Luchins, D. J. and Perline, R. 1984. Facial affect recognition in schizophrenia: Is there a differential deficit? *British Journal of Psychiatry* 144: 533–537.

Nummenmaa, T. 1964. *The Language of the Face*. University of Jyvaskyla Studies in Education, Psychology and Social Research, No. 9.

Odom, P., Blanton, R., and Laukhuf, C. 1973. Facial expressions and interpretations of emotion-arousing situations in deaf and hearing children. *Journal of Abnormal Child Psychology* 1: 139–151.

Oswald, D., and Ollendick, T. 1989. Role taking and social competence in autism and mental retardation. *Journal of Autism and Developmental Disorders* 19: 119–128.

Ozonoff, S. In press. Executive functions in autism. In *Learning and Cognition in Autism*, ed. E. Schopler and G. Mesibov. Plenum.

Ozonoff, S., Pennington, B., and Rogers, S. 1990. Are there emotion perception deficits in young autistic children? *Journal of Child Psychology and Psychiatry* 31: 343–363.

Ozonoff, S., Pennington, B., and Rogers, S. 1991. Executive function deficits in high-functioning autistic children: Relationship to theory of mind. *Journal of Child Psychology and Psychiatry* 32: 1081–1106.

Ozonoff, S., Rogers, S., and Pennington, B. 1991. Asperger's Syndrome: Evidence of an empirical distinction from high-functioning autism. *Journal of Child Psychology and Psychiatry* 32: 1107–1122.

Papousek, H., and Papousek, M. 1979. Early ontogeny of human social interaction: Its biological roots and social dimensions. In *Human Ethology: Claims and Limits of a New Discipline*, ed. M. von Cranach et al. Cambridge University Press.

Perner, J. 1991. *Understanding the Representational Mind*. MIT Press.

Perner, J. 1993. The theory of mind deficit in autism: Rethinking the metarepresentation theory. In *Understanding Other Minds: Perspectives from Autism*, ed. S. Baron-Cohen et al. Oxford University Press.

Perner, J. and Wimmer, H. 1985. "John thinks that Mary thinks that . . .": Attribution of second-order beliefs by 5–10 year old children. *Journal of Experimental Child Psychology* 39: 437–471.

Perner, J., Frith, U., Leslie, A., and Leekam, S. 1989. Exploration of the autistic child's theory of mind: Knowledge, belief, and communication. *Child Development* 60: 689–700.

Perrett, D., and Mistlin, A. 1990. Perception of facial characteristics by monkeys. In *Comparative Perception*, volume 2: *Complex Signals*, ed. W. Stebbins and M. Berkely. Wiley.

Perrett, D., Rolls, E., and Cann, W. 1982. Visual neurones responsive to faces in the monkey temporal cortex. *Experimental Brain Research* 47: 329–342.

Perrett, D., Smith, P., Potter, D., Mistlin, A., Head, A., Milner, A., and Jeeves, M. 1985. Visual cells in the temporal cortex sensitive to face view and gaze direction. *Proceedings of the Royal Society of London* B 223: 293–317.

Perrett, D., Harries, M., Mistlin, A., Hietanen, J., Benson, P., Bevan, R., Thomas, S., Oram, M., Ortega, J., and Brierley, K. 1990. Social signals analyzed at the single cell level: Someone is looking at me, something touched me, something moved! *International Journal of Comparative Psychology* 4: 25–55.

Perrett, D., Hietanen, M., Oram, W., and Benson, P. 1991. Organization and function of cells responsive to faces in the temporal cortex. *Philosophical Transactions of the Royal Society of London* B 335: 1–128.

Phillips, W. 1993. Understanding Intention and Desire by Children with Autism. Ph.D. thesis, Institute of Psychiatry, University of London.

Phillips, W., Baron-Cohen, S., and Rutter, M. 1992. The role of eye-contact in the detection of goals: Evidence from normal toddlers, and children with autism or mental handicap. *Development and Psychopathology* 4: 375–383.

Pinker, S. 1994. *The Language Instinct*. Penguin.

Piven, J., Berthier, M., Starkstein, S. Nehme, E., Pearlson, G., and Folstein, S. 1990. Magnetic resonance imaging evidence for a defect of cerebral cortical development in autism. *American Journal of Psychiatry* 147: 737–739.

Porrino, L., Crane, A., and Goldman-Rakic, P. 1982. Direct and indirect pathways from the amygdala to the frontal lobe in rhesus monkeys. *Journal of Comparative Neurology* 198: 121–136.

Povinelli, D., and Eddy, T. 1994. Comments on target article by Baron-Cohen [1994b above].

Povinelli, D., and Eddy, T. In press. *What Young Chimpanzees Know about Seeing*. Society for Research in Child Development.

Povinelli, D., Parks, K., and Novak, M. 1991. Do Rhesus monkeys (*Macaca mulatta*) attribute knowledge and ignorance to others? *Journal of Comparative Psychology* 105: 318–325.

Pratt, C., and Bryant, P. 1990. Young children understand that looking leads to knowing (so long as they are looking into a single barrel). *Child Development* 61: 973–983.

Premack, D. 1988. `Does the chimpanzee have a theory of mind?' revisited. In *Machiavellian Intelligence: Social Expertise and the Evolution of Intellect.*, ed. R. Byrne and A. Whiten. Oxford University Press.

Premack, D. 1990. Do infants have a theory of self-propelled objects? *Cognition* 36: 1–16.

Premack, D. 1993. Invited lecture, MRC Cognitive Development Unit/University College London, November.

Premack, D., and Dasser, V. 1991. Theory of mind in apes and children. In *Natural Theories of Mind*, ed. A. Whiten. Blackwell.

Premack, D., and Woodruff, G. 1978. Does the chimpanzee have a "theory of mind"? *Behavior and Brain Sciences* 4: 515–526.

Price, B., Daffner, K., Stowe, R., and Mesulam, M. 1990. The compartmental learning disabilities of early frontal lobe damage. *Brain* 113: 1383–1393.

Prior, M., and Hammond, W. 1990. Neuropsychological testing of autistic children through exploration with frontal lobe tests. *Journal of Autism and Developmental Disorders* 20: 581–590.

Prior, M., Dahlstrom, B., and Squires, T. 1990. Autistic children's knowledge of thinking and feeling states in other people. *Journal of Child Psychology and Psychiatry* 31: 587–602.

Reddy, V. 1991. Playing with other's expectations: Teasing and mucking about in the first year. In *Natural Theories of Mind*, ed. A. Whiten. Blackwell.

Reed, T. and Peterson, C. 1990. A comparative study of autistic subjects' performance at two levels of visual and cognitive perspective taking. *Journal of Autism and Developmental Disorders* 20: 555–568.

Ristau, C. 1990. Aspects of the cognitive ethology of an injury feigning plover. In *Cognitive Ethology: The Minds of Other Animals*, ed. C. Ristau. Erlbaum.

Ristau, C. 1991. Attention, purposes, and deception in birds. In *Natural Theories of Mind*, ed. A. Whiten. Blackwell.

Rogers, S., and Pennington, B. 1991. A theoretical approach to the deficit in infantile autism. *Development and Psychopathology* 3: 137–162.

Roth, D., and Leslie, A. 1991. The recognition of attitude conveyed by utterance: A study of preschool and autistic children. *British Journal of Developmental Psychology* 9: 315–330.

Rubin, A. 1970. Measurement of romantic love. *Journal of Personal and Social Psychology* 16: 265–273.

Rutter, M. 1978. Language disorder and infantile autism. In *Autism: A Reappraisal of Concepts and Treatment*, ed. M. Rutter and E. Schopler. Plenum.

Rutter, M., and Bailey, A. 1993. Thinking and relationships: Mind and brain (some reflections on theory of mind and autism). In *Understanding Other Minds: Perspectives from Autism*, ed. S. Baron-Cohen et al. Oxford University Press.

Sacks, O. 1994. A neurologist's notebook: An anthropologist on Mars. *New Yorker*, December 27, 1993–January 3, 1994.

Samuels, C. 1985. Attention to eye contact opportunity and facial motion by 3 month old infants. *Journal of Experimental Child Psychology* 40: 105–114.

Scaife, M. 1976. The response to eye-like shapes by birds. II. The importance of staring, pairedness, and shape. *Animal Behavior* 24: 200–206.

Scaife, M., and Bruner, J. 1975. The capacity for joint visual attention in the infant. *Nature* 253: 265–266.

Schaffer, H. 1977. Early interactive development. In *Studies in Mother-Infant Interaction*, ed. H. Schaffer. Academic Press.

Schaller, G. 1964. *The Mountain Gorilla*. University of Chicago Press.

Shah, A. and Frith, U. 1983. An islet of ability in autism: A research note. *Journal of Child Psychology and Psychiatry* 24: 613–620.

Shah, A., and Frith, U. 1993. Why do autistic individuals show superior performance on the block design test? *Journal of Child Psychology and Psychiatry* 34: 1351–1364.

Sodian, B. 1991. The development of deception in young children. *British Journal of Developmental Psychology* 9: 173–188.

Sodian, B., and Frith, U. 1992. Deception and sabotage in autistic, retarded, and normal children. *Journal of Child Psychology and Psychiatry* 33: 591–606.

Sodian, B., and Frith, U. 1993. The theory of mind deficit in autism: Evidence from deception. In *Understanding Other Minds: Perspectives from Autism*, ed. S. Baron-Cohen et al. Oxford University Press.

Sodian, B., Taylor, C., Harris, P., and Perner, J 1992. Early deception and the child's theory of mind: False trails and genuine markers. *Child Development* 62: 468–483.

Sorce, J., Emde, R., Campos, J., and Klinnert, M. 1985. Maternal emotional signalling: Its effect on the visual cliff behavior of 1 year olds. *Developmental Psychology* 21: 195–200.

Sperber, D. 1993. Paper presented at conference on Darwin and the Human Sciences, London School of Economics, June.

Sperber, D., and Wilson, D. 1986. *Relevance: Communication and Cognition*. Blackwell.

Spitz, R. 1946. The smiling response: A contribution to the ontogenesis of social relations. *Genetic Psychology Monographs* 34: 57–125.

Stern, D. 1977. *The First Relationship: Infant and Mother*. Harvard University Press.

Stern, D. 1985. *The Interpersonal World of the Infant*. Basic Books.

Stevenson, B. 1946. *Stevenson's Book of Quotations*, fifth edition. Cassell.

Swettenham, J. 1992. The Autistic Child's Theory of Mind: A Computer-Based Investigation. Ph.D. thesis, University of York.

Tager-Flusberg, H. 1989. A psycholinguistic perspective on language development in the autistic child. In *Autism: Nature, Diagnosis, and Treatment*, ed. G. Dawson. Guilford.

Tager-Flusberg, H. 1993. What language reveals about the understanding of minds in children with autism. In *Understanding Other Minds: Perspectives from Autism*, ed. S. Baron-Cohen et al. Oxford University Press.

Tan, J., and Harris, P. 1991. Autistic children understand seeing and wanting. *Development and Psychopathology* 3: 163–174.

Tantam, D. 1992. Characterizing the fundamental social handicap in autism. *Acta Paedopsychiatrica* 55: 88–91.

Tantam, D., Monaghan, L., Nicholson, H., and Stirling, J. 1989. Autistic children's ability to interpret faces: A research note. *Journal of Child Psychology and Psychiatry* 30: 623–630.

Thayer, S. 1977. Children's detection of on-face and off-face gazes. *Developmental Psychology* 13: 673–674.

Thayer, S., and Schiff, W. 1977. Gazing patterns and attribution of sexual involvement. *Journal of Social Psychology* 101: 235–246.

Tinbergen, N. 1951. *The Study of Instinct*. Oxford University Press.

Tomasello, M. 1988. The role of joint-attentional processes in early language acquisition. *Language Sciences* 10: 69–88.

Tooby, J., and Cosmides, L. 1992. The psychological foundations of culture. In *The Adapted Mind*, ed. J. Barkow et al. Oxford University Press.

Trevarthen, C. 1979. Communication and cooperation in early infancy: A description of primary intersubjectivity. In *Before Speech*, ed. M. Bullowa. Cambridge University Press.

Trevarthen, C. and Hubley, P. 1978. Secondary intersubjectivity: Confidence, confiders, and acts of meaning in the first year. In *Before Speech: The Beginning of Interpersonal Communication*, ed. A. Lock. Academic Press.

Ungerer, J., and Sigman, M. 1981. Symbolic play and language comprehension in autistic children. *Journal of the American Academy of Child Psychiatry* 20: 318–337.

Van Hoesen, G. 1981. The differential distribution, diversity, and sprouting of cortical projections to the amygdala in the rhesus monkey. In *The Amygdaloid Complex*, ed. Y. Ben-Ari. Elsevier.

Van Hooff, J. 1962. Facial expressions in higher primates. *Symposium of the Zoological Society of London* 8: 97–125.

Vicera, S., and Johnson, M. Gaze detection and the cortical processing of faces: Evidence from infants and adults. *Visual Cognition*, in press.

Vine, I. 1973. The role of facial signalling in early social development. In *Social Communication and Movement: Studies of Men and Chimpanzees*, ed. M. von Cranach and I. Vine. Academic Press.

Volkmar, F., and Cohen, D. 1989. Disintegrative disorder or "late onset" autism? *Journal of Child Psychology and Psychiatry* 30: 717–724.

Volkmar, F., and Mayes, L. 1990. Gaze behavior in autism. *Development and Psychopathology* 2: 61–69.

Wada, J. 1961. Modification of cortically induced responses in brainstem by shift of attention in monkeys. *Science* 133: 40–42.

Warrington, E., and Shallice, T. 1984. Category specific semantic impairments. *Brain* 107: 829–854.

Wellman, H. 1985. The child's theory of mind: The development of conceptions of cognition. In *The Growth of Reflection in Children*, ed. S. Yussen. Academic Press.

Wellman, H. 1990. *The Child's Theory of Mind*. MIT Press.

Wellman, H., and Estes, D. 1986. Early understanding of mental entities: A reexamination of childhood realism. *Child Development* 57: 910–923.

Whiten, A. 1991. *Natural Theories of Mind*. Blackwell.

Whiten, A., and Perner, J. 1991. Fundamental issues in the multidisciplinary study of mindreading. In *Natural Theories of Mind*, ed. A. Whiten. Blackwell.

Wimmer, H., and Perner, J. 1983. Beliefs about beliefs: Representation and constraining function of wrong beliefs in young children's understanding of deception. *Cognition* 13: 103–128.

Wing, L. 1976. *Early Childhood Autism*. Pergamon.

Wolff, P. 1963. Observations on the early development of smiling. In *Determinants of Infant Behavior*, volume 2, ed. B. Foss. Wiley.

Yirmiya, N., Sigman, M., Kasari, C., and Mundy, P. 1992. Empathy and cognition in high functioning children with autism. *Child Development* 63: 150–160.

Zeki, S. 1993. *A Vision of the Brain*. Blackwell.

Index